Horn pd

STEPPING-STONES

D0104780

STEPPING-STONES
A New Testament Guide for Beginners

Peter Jeffery

The Banner of Truth Trust

THE BANNER OF TRUTH TRUST
3 Murrayfield Road, Edinburgh EH12 6EL
PO Box 621, Carlisle, Pennsylvania 17013, USA

★

© Peter Jeffery 1991
First Published 1991
ISBN 0 85151 597 5

★

Typeset in 10½/12pt. Linotron Plantin at
The Spartan Press Limited, Lymington, Hants
Reproduced, printed and bound in Great Britain by
Courier International, Glasgow

TO JONATHAN, CHRISTOPHER & REBECCA

CONTENTS

INTRODUCTION

The word 'Bible' comes from the Greek word biblia, meaning 'books'. The Bible is a collection of 66 books written by about 40 men over a period of 1500 years. Each of these books is different from the others, written at a particular time for a particular reason, but they are all necessary to each other if we are to have a full understanding of the truth of God. The Bible is God's revealed truth. It records what God has said and done concerning our salvation. Like stepping-stones across a stream, each book is needed if we are to cross safely from spiritual darkness and ignorance into the light of the truth of God.

It is possible to come to a saving faith in the Lord Jesus Christ with a very limited knowledge of the Bible, but if the saved person is to grow in the Christian faith, he needs to know and benefit from all that God has revealed to us in inspired Scripture. If you were crossing a stream on stepping-stones and found in the middle that a few of the stones were missing, you would be in trouble. Thank God that none of His stepping-stones is missing. We have a complete Bible, but if we ignore some books of Scripture, or if ignorance of their teaching is left untreated, it is as if some of the stepping-stones have been removed and we will then be in spiritual trouble. We need all the Bible for a healthy spiritual life.

This book is written as a guide to the 27 stepping-stones which we call the New Testament. It is written primarily for those new to the Christian faith, but it is hoped that it will also help those who have been Christians for several years to understand more clearly the background, structure and content of each of the New Testament books. I have tried to be brief, simple and accurate. This is not meant to be a deep or exhaustive study of the New

Testament but an introductory help to those young in the faith. It is hoped that an understanding of the New Testament will create a desire for more understanding of the Old Testament, and thus all of God's truth will be our delight.

The New Testament is only a part of the Bible and to fully understand its teaching the Old Testament is necessary, so whilst in this book our concern is with the New Testament, do not neglect the Old.

The Bible verses quoted are from the New International Version.

The Four Gospels

The word 'gospel' means 'good news', and in the New Testament has a general reference to what God has done to save sinners in and through the life and death of the Lord Jesus Christ. Nowhere is the word applied to a specific book. When we speak, for instance, of the Gospel of Mark, we must understand that it means the good news of the Lord Jesus Christ as recorded by Mark. See Mark 1:1, which illustrates the truth of this. Having said that, however, we have to acknowledge that from the very earliest time in the history of the Christian Church, the term 'gospel' has been applied to the four books at the beginning of the New Testament which record for us the life of Christ. Probably as early as AD125 the four books were brought together and so used by the Church.

In the strict meaning of the word, there is only ONE gospel, but there are four distinct accounts of all those events and teachings which comprise the gospel. Why do we need four separate presentations of one gospel? The answer to that is found in the reason the four books were written. The writers did not set out to write detailed biographies. Their purpose was to show us Jesus as the eternal Son of God, whom God sent into the world to die as an atonement for sins. This is why one may omit what another includes and why the order of events does not always tally. The writers were not biographers but proclaimers of the gospel and we need all four to give us a full and accurate portrait of the person and work of the Lord Jesus Christ. Obviously, there are differences in the four Gospels, but that does not affect the question of the authority and inspiration of the books. While every word of the Bible is inspired by God, it is expressed through different men with different styles and thought-forms. The Holy Spirit did not suppress the personality of the writers but used it (1 Corinthians 2:13).

Inspiration is not mechanical, so when Matthew, Mark, Luke and John record for us events in the life of Jesus, they do so from the viewpoint from which they saw them. If four witnesses in court all gave evidence of a certain event in exactly the same words, then the judge would probably conclude that they had got together beforehand and agreed what to say. But if each man spoke in his own words, with his own emphasis, then the evidence would be stronger, even though not identical. That is what we have in the four Gospels – each man tells the same story in his own way.

Dates and Order

Though Matthew is the first book in the New Testament, it was not the first to be written. It will be helpful to see the order in which the New Testament books were written. The following is a possible order, though it is impossible to be specific about dates.

AD 40–50	JAMES
AD 50–54	GALATIANS, I & 2 THESSALONIANS
AD 55–60	I & 2 CORINTHIANS, ROMANS, MARK
AD 60–65	COLOSSIANS, PHILEMON, EPHESIANS, PHILIPPIANS
AD 65–70	I & 2 TIMOTHY, TITUS, JUDE, HEBREWS, I & 2 PETER, MATTHEW, LUKE, ACTS
AD 90–	JOHN, I, 2 & 3 JOHN, REVELATION

Matthew was probably put first when the New Testament was brought together because it is the natural link with the Old Testament. Matthew was writing with the Jews particularly in mind and he quotes from the Old Testament 53 times, compared with 36 quotes in Mark, 25 in Luke and 20 in John.

If the order of writing above is correct, then Mark was the first of the four Gospels to be written. This means that the other three Gospel writers would have had Mark to refer to when they wrote. William Hendriksen tells us: 'One finds, upon examination, that Matthew's Gospel contains, in substance, almost all of the Gospel according to Mark; in fact, of Mark's 661 verses as many as 606 (= about eleven-twelfths) are paralleled in Matthew. Also, slightly more than half of Mark (350 verses – about 53%) is reproduced in Luke.' Hendriksen goes on to say: 'It is not hard to believe, therefore, that Matthew, in harmony with his own distinctive plan, used it, enlarged on it, and added much material, both from his own experience and from other sources. And should we not be grateful that such unity of spirit was present among the Gospel writers that both Matthew and Luke were delighted to use Mark's Gospel, each of these two using it in his own way?'

The similarity between the first three Gospels has caused them to be known as the Synoptic Gospels. 'Synoptic' means 'viewed together'. As they are studied side by side it becomes apparent that they have much material in common.

John's Gospel was the last to be written, and it goes deeper than the others into the meaning and significance of the life and death of Jesus. 'In distinction from the Synoptics, John's Gospel discusses not so much the kingdom as the King Himself, reveals that Jesus from the very beginning asserted His Messianic claim; describes, with few exceptions, Christ's work in Judea; dwells at great length on the events and discourses which belong to a period of less than twenty-four hours; unmistakably indicates that the active ministry of our Lord extended over a period of at least three years; and, in general, places great emphasis upon the spiritual character of Christ's task on earth. Nevertheless, John and the Synoptics, far from contradicting each other, supplement each other' (William Hendriksen).

The value of these four Gospels is spoken of by David Brown in these words: 'The Fourfold Gospel is the central portion of Divine Revelation. Into it, as a Reservoir, all the foregoing revelations pour their full tide, and out of it, as a Fountain, flow all subsequent revelations. In other parts of Scripture we hear Christ by the hearing of the ear; but here our eye seeth Him. Elsewhere we see Him through a glass darkly; but here, face to face.'

ᏇᏇ 2 ᏇᏇ

Matthew

The first Gospel does not tell us who wrote it, but from very early on the Church believed that its author was the apostle Matthew, whose conversion is described for us in Matthew 9:9–13. In the parallel passages in Mark and Luke (Mark 2:14 & Luke 5:27–28), he is called Levi. He was a tax-collector, that is, a Jew working for the hated Romans and consequently unpopular with his fellow Jews. But in his Gospel, Matthew had the Jews particularly in mind. He writes to convince his fellow Jews that Jesus is the Messiah, the Christ. Thus, he quotes extensively from the Old Testament. The phrase in 1:22, 'All this took place to fulfil what the Lord had said through the prophet', is repeated many times as he seeks to convince Jews who were very familiar with the Old Testament that Jesus was the fulfilment of the old prophecies.

Spurgeon, commenting on the first verse of Matthew, said: 'This verse gives us a clue to the special drift of Matthew's Gospel. He was moved of the Holy Spirit to write of our Lord Jesus Christ as King – "the son of David". He is to be spoken of as specially reigning over the true seed of Abraham; hence he is called "the son of Abraham". Lord Jesus, make us each one to call thee, "My God and King!" As we read this wonderful Gospel of the Kingdom, may we be full of loyal obedience, and pay thee humble homage! Thou art both King and a king's Son.'

For Matthew, Jesus is the true King. 'So Matthew is careful to record what Jesus said about his kingdom – the kingdom of heaven. He gives us a great deal of Jesus's teaching . . . These alternate with sections of narrative in the Gospel, and include the famous "Sermon on the Mount". Matthew's Gospel, more than any other, is the link between the Old Testament and the New, the old Israel and the new world-wide church of God's people' (*The Lion Handbook*).

CONTENTS

SUMMARY

In the first three-and-a-half chapters (up to 4:11), Matthew sets before us the significant human ancestry of Jesus. Remember that he is writing to Jews who had rejected Jesus as the Messiah. The genealogy lists the ancestors of Jesus right back to Abraham. Matthew seeks to show that 'Jesus is the son of David, and the son of Abraham: He is the culmination of the divine promise' (Gresham Machen).

It is interesting that Matthew does not actually record the birth of Jesus. The passage in 1:18–25 is, like the genealogy, dealing with the origins of Jesus, and it is done to show the fulfilment of the prophecy of Isaiah 7. The supernatural origin of Jesus is crucial for our salvation. 'The rejection of Christ's supernatural origin leaves his supernatural life and deeds unexplained. It also leaves unexplained the very possibility of man's salvation. That salvation is secured only when the initiative is taken by God, not by man!' (William Hendriksen).

The Jews may well reject Jesus but certain Gentiles do not, and notice again in chapter two the fulfilment of Old Testament prophecies in v.6 and v.8. The baptism and temptation of Jesus once more emphasize his uniqueness. Heaven (3:17) and hell (4:6) both testify that this is no ordinary man. 'We have Him divinely attested by Him who knew Him best and cannot lie; and thus publicly inaugurated, formally installed in all the authority of His mediatorial office, as the Son of God in the flesh, and the Object of His Father's absolute complacency' (David Brown).

The ministry of Jesus begins in 4:12. Note that the first recorded message of Jesus is on repentance (4:17). Repentance is also the first subject dealt with by John the Baptist (3:2), Peter (Acts 2:38), and Paul (Acts 26:20). The purpose of the Gospel is not simply to teach men facts about God, but to convict us of our sin and call us to repentance. Only after such conviction will our sins be forgiven, as we are brought in faith to know God as our Lord and Saviour and King.

Matthew brings us the teaching of Jesus both in particular sayings and in extended passages. The first of the latter is the Sermon on the Mount (chapters 5–7).

'In the Sermon on the Mount Jesus is contrasting the laws of the kingdom especially with the laws promulgated by the Pharisees. The contrast has often been misinterpreted. Men have represented Jesus as a mild philanthropist who mitigated the severities of Moses. There could be no more complete reversal of the facts. Such misinterpretation is guarded against by Jesus himself. "Except your righteousness shall exceed the righteousness of the scribes and Pharisees, ye shall in no wise enter into the kingdom of heaven." Matthew 5:20. With all their insistence upon minute details, the Pharisees were really advocating, not too strict an interpretation of the law of Moses, but an interpretation not nearly strict enough. The Pharisees were satisfied with obedience to a set of external rules; Jesus demanded purity of heart. Jesus came not to make things easier, but to make things harder . . . Without the cross, the Sermon on the Mount would be an intolerable burden: with the cross, it becomes the guide to a way of life. In the Sermon on the Mount, Jesus has held up an unattainable ideal, he has revealed the depths of human guilt, he has made demands far too lofty for human strength. But, thank God, he has revealed guilt only to wash it away, and with his demands he has given strength to fulfil them' (J. Gresham Machen).

Chapters 8–16 deal mainly with the general ministry of Jesus in Galilee. Here we see the power of Jesus in healings and other miracles like calming the storm and feeding the crowds. Chapter 13 is full of parables concerning the kingdom of heaven. The teaching and the miracles astound the crowd but it does not lead to faith (13:53–58). Matthew has been presenting in this section a series of incidents that reveal the truth that Jesus is indeed the Messiah. But while people remain unbelieving, they are forced to ask the question: Who is this man? Some held a very lofty opinion of Jesus (16:13–14), but it is left to Simon Peter finally to put the truth into words, 'You are the Christ (the Messiah), the Son of the living God' (16:16).

The truth of this statement is further confirmed in the next chapter in the account of the transfiguration.

The remainder of chapter 17 and chapter 18 deal with the last of Christ's ministry in Galilee. He then leaves the north and proceeds south on his way to Jerusalem and the cross. On this journey the Saviour once again prepares the apostles for what is about to happen (20:17–19). He has done this twice before (16:21 and 17:22–23) but now for the first time he tells them that he is to be crucified. 'The effect is to emphasize not only the totality of the rejection (Jewish leaders and Gentiles), but also the humiliation and the harrowing pain; this is to be no glorious martyrdom, but an ugly, sordid butchery. It is thus all the more striking to read yet again here that he will be raised on the third day; the contrast, and the miraculous power which creates it, are more marked than ever. Chapter 20, verse 28 will go on to explain the paradox: this apparently tragic death is in fact an act of service, a source of life for "many"' (R. T. France).

At this point the apostles are not told what they afterwards come to see so clearly, namely, that the suffering and death of Christ were divinely imposed. See Acts 2:23.

The last week of Christ's earthly life begins in chapter 21 with the triumphal entry into Jerusalem, which Matthew is quick to remind us is a fulfilment of the prophecy of Zechariah 9:9. The teaching of the last week was particularly challenging and Christ's denunciation of those who reject him was very severe (21:31–32). But still the seven woes of chapter 23 end with a lament of deep compassion (vv.37–39). 'What a combination of withering denunciation and weeping lamentation do we find here – as if the intensity of the Redeemer's holy emotions, in their most vivid contrast, had only found full vent at this last visit to Jerusalem, and in this His last public address to the impenitent nation. And if the verses which conclude this chapter were indeed His last words to

[7]

them, as it is evident they were, how worthy were they of Him, and of the awful occasion, and how pregnant with warning to every such favoured region' (David Brown).

The remaining chapters (26–28) deal with the culmination of all the Old Testament prophecies. This is why Jesus came into the world. The death of Jesus was no tragic end in which circumstances and the plots of enemies triumphed. All the way through, Jesus is in charge, and God's will is being done. That does not lessen the guilt of Judas, Caiaphas, Pilate and the rest of the plotters. 'Thus God's saving design and man's malevolence are here woven together into an immensely powerful drama, which will conclude in ch.28 with the ultimate triumph of Jesus as the risen Lord of all' (R. T. France).

The triumph of the Lord Jesus Christ is brought out vividly, yet simply, in 28:2. Matthew Henry says of this verse: 'He came, and rolled back the stone from the door, and sat upon it. Our Lord Jesus could have rolled back the stone himself by his own power, but he chose to have it done by an angel, to signify that having undertaken to make satisfaction for our sin, imputed to him, and being under arrest pursuant to that imputation, he did not break prison, but an officer was sent on purpose to roll away the stone, and so to open the prison door, which would never have been done, if He had not made a full satisfaction . . . The angel's sitting upon the stone, when he had rolled it away, is very observable, and bespeaks of a secure triumph over all the obstructions of Christ's resurrection. There he sat, defying all the powers of hell to roll the stone to the grave again.'

STUDY MATERIAL

Expository thoughts on the Gospels – Matthew by J. C. Ryle (Banner of Truth, 1986).
The Four Gospels by David Brown (Banner of Truth, 1976).
The Sermon on the Mount by Sinclair Ferguson (Banner of Truth, 1987).

෮ 3 ෮

Mark

Like the first Gospel, Mark does not mention the name of its author, but tradition from very early in Church history ascribes this second Gospel to Mark. The same tradition tells us that Mark was dependent for his information upon the Apostle Peter. 'Moreover, the contents of the book confirm this conclusion. Peter's sins and weaknesses are recorded faithfully, but the praise which he received elsewhere (for example in Matt. 16:17) is omitted from Mark. Again, at times Mark mentions Peter by name (5:37; 11:21; 16:7) when Matthew does not. Mark's Gospel, moreover, is characterized by a certain vividness, rapidity of movement, and attention to detail, which characteristics are easily associated with active, vivacious, enthusiastic Peter' (William Hendriksen).

There are several references in Acts and the Epistles to Mark. His mother's home was a centre of Christian life and activity in Jerusalem (Acts 12:12). His first Christian work was as helper to Paul and Barnabas (Acts 12:25). He accompanied these two men on their first missionary journey but returned prematurely to Jerusalem (Acts 13:13). This upset Paul, who refused to take John Mark on the second journey (Acts 15:36–41). The rift was not permanent and during Paul's first imprisonment in Rome, Mark was with him (Col. 4:10). Later it appears that Mark became a companion of Peter, and this apostle speaks of him very warmly (1 Pet. 5:13).

Mark was probably writing for gentiles, and hence there is nothing like the number of Old Testament quotations that we find in Matthew. When he refers to Jewish customs, of which the Romans would have no understanding, Mark explains them (7:2–4; 5:42). For the same reason, Aramaic words are translated (3:17;

[9]

5:41). The book is taken up, not so much with the words of Jesus – there are few parables – but with Christ's actions.

Though the book is much shorter than Matthew, it contains almost as many of the miracles of Jesus. Several of these miracles are related in more detail in Mark than the other Gospels. 'As in Matthew Jesus appears as a teacher, so in Mark he is presented as a worker. In the Second Gospel, it is the power of Jesus, manifested in wonderful deeds of mercy, which is in the foreground. Of course the difference between Matthew and Mark must not be exaggerated. Both sides of the ministry of Jesus appear clearly in both Gospels; the difference is at most a difference of emphasis' (Gresham Machen).

Gresham Machen also describes Mark as the Missionary Gospel. He says: 'It contains only those things which had a place in the first preaching to unbelievers . . . Hence the omission of the mystery of the birth, of the profound teaching of the early Judean ministry, of the intimate instructions to the disciples. These things are of fundamental importance. But they can best be understood only after one has first acquired a thorough grasp of the public ministry, and of the death and resurrection of the Lord.'

CONTENTS

SUMMARY

After a very brief treatment of the baptism and temptation of Jesus, Mark goes straight to the actions of the Saviour. Chapter one is full of activity, which includes preaching, calling disciples, casting out evil spirits and healing the sick. But effective activity in the work of God, even for the Lord Jesus Christ, necessitated a period of being alone with God in prayer (1:35). In his own actions and instructions to others, Jesus always put a great emphasis on prayer (Mark 9:29; 13:33; 14:38).

It is interesting and significant that Mark shows us the importance of prayer in the earthly life of Jesus at a time when the Lord is surrounded by popular adoration (2:1–2) and the beginnings of a vigorous opposition (2:6, 16, 24; 3:2). The opposition 'comes to a head when the deputation from Jerusalem, sent to look into His activities, ascribe His expulsion of demons to the energizing power of Beelzebul, which brings upon them His solemn warning of the danger of sinning against the Holy Spirit, that deliberate shutting of their eyes to the light which was by its very nature irremediable' (*The New Bible Handbook*).

There are very few parables in Mark, yet four are gathered together in chapter four. This is fitting after the opposition of chapters two and three. In spite of the blindness and antagonism of the Jewish religious leaders, nothing will stop the seed of divine truth from growing, and the teaching ministry goes on. The next few chapters are taken up with the ministry around the Sea of Galilee. The demonstration of the power of the Lord Jesus was awesome, yet it was not always popular and sometimes for reasons that caused the Lord to be amazed at their lack of faith. This is again seen in Nazareth (6:1–6). 'In Jesus' home town it is not a case of "local boy makes good" but "who does this jumped up carpenter think he is?"' (*The Lion Handbook*).

In spite of this, the ministry expands and Jesus sends out the twelve apostles, two by two, to preach and heal. This was a period in the three-year ministry of Jesus of great popular response. The crowds who came to hear Him were enormous and their keenness was so marked that they often neglected necessary food. On two separate occasions Jesus used His divine power to feed them (6:30–44, 8:1–9).

From Galilee Jesus goes north to Tyre, then south again to Decapolis, back to Bethsaida in Galilee and north again to Caesarea Philippi. Thus, Mark portrays the great energy and activity of Jesus. His ministry only lasted three years but there was not a wasted moment.

The Galilean ministry concludes in chapter nine, with the solemn warning of vv. 42–50. 'This is a rule that sounds stern and harsh at first sight. But our loving Master did not give the rule without cause. Compliance with it is absolutely necessary, since neglect of it is the sure way to hell. Our bodily senses are the channels through which many of our most formidable temptations approach us. Our bodily members are ready instruments of evil, but slow to that which is good. The eye, the hand, and the foot are good servants, when under right direction. But they need daily watching, lest they lead us into sin' (J. C. Ryle).

Jesus now sets his face towards Jerusalem and the cross, as He moves south from Galilee to Judea. The crowds come to Him, but so do the Pharisees with their trick question (10:2). It is clear now that the cross is dominating the thinking of Jesus (10:32–34), but the apostles are preoccupied with other things. But although the disciples may have failed to understand the passion-prediction, yet at least something in the Lord's manner warned them that the hour of the establishment of His kingdom was near; and so each disciple is quick to strike for his own hand. 'Ironically enough, although the request of the "Thunderers" was wrong-headed, yet at least it denoted faith in Christ's ability to establish His kingdom. So the Lord dealt gently with them, more gently than the ten would have dealt, as we see from 10: 41ff. The petty selfishness of His followers at a time like this, when His mind was full of all that lay ahead at Jerusalem, must have cut Him to the quick; but compare their sleep in the Garden of Gethsemane (14:37). Are we, today, blind also?' (R. Alan Cole).

The last week of the Saviour's life is dealt with in the remaining chapters. Out of 16 chapters, Mark takes 6 to describe the last days of Jesus. The same is true of the other three Gospel writers. Matthew takes 8 chapters out of 28; Luke 5 out of 24 and John 10 out of 21. Here is the greatest and ultimate action of the Lord Jesus as He gives His life a ransom for many.

STUDY MATERIAL

Expository thoughts on the Gospels – Mark by J. C. Ryle (Banner of Truth, 1986).

∾ 4 ∾

Luke

Once again, as in the first two Gospels, there is no statement to tell us who wrote this book. But we do know to whom it was written. Like the Acts of the Apostles, it was written to a man named Theophilus. It is reasonable, therefore, to assume that whoever wrote Acts also wrote Luke, because Acts 1:1 says that it is a continuation of an earlier book about Jesus, addressed to the same person. So who wrote Acts? Whoever it was was with Paul at Philippi. Note the use of the personal pronoun 'we' in Acts 16:10–13. This narrows the field down, and from evidence such as this and an early Christian tradition there seems little doubt that the author was the man Paul called 'our dear friend Luke, the doctor' (Col. 4:14).

Luke and Acts were two books written by the same man to give a carefully researched (Luke 1:3–4) and accurate history of the Christian faith. Luke was a gentile writing particularly for gentiles like Theophilus. Here we have the fullest life story of Jesus in what is the longest book in the New Testament. 'The historical method of the author appears not only in the completeness and accuracy and orderly arrangement of the work, but also in the success with which Luke has brought the events that he narrates into connection with secular history. In the elaborate dating of the beginning of John the Baptist's ministry, Luke 3:1,2, and in the numerous other references to imperial officials which are peculiar to the Third Gospel and The Acts, Luke has revealed himself as a citizen of the world and as a genuine Greek historian. It is well, in the interests of a complete picture, that one of the four Gospels was written not by a Jew but by a Greek' (J. Gresham Machen).

If in Matthew we see Jesus as King, and in Mark we see the actions and power of Jesus, in Luke the emphasis is on the love of

[13]

the Saviour. 'An important part of God's concern for people is that it is manifested towards groups not highly esteemed in first-century society: women, children, the poor, the disreputable. He gives a significant place to women. In the first century women were kept very much in their place, but Luke sees them as the objects of God's love and he writes about many of them' (Leon Morris).

CONTENTS

SUMMARY

Luke gives us by far the longest and most detailed account of the birth of Jesus, and only he mentions the event in the temple when Jesus was twelve years old. 'In this section of his Gospel, Luke shows himself to be a genuine historian. A biographer is not satisfied with narrating the public life of his hero, but prefaces to his work some account of the family, and of the birth and childhood. So our understanding of the ministry of Jesus becomes far deeper when we know that he grew up among simple, devout folk who are described in the first two chapters of Luke. The picture of Mary in these chapters, painted with an exquisite delicacy of touch, throws a flood of light upon the earthly life of the Son of Man' (J. Gresham Machen).

Matthew's and Luke's account of the birth of Christ differ greatly in detail and incident, but both agree on what is the heart of the message. Jesus was born of a virgin (Matt. 1:23, Luke 1:34) and the purpose of his birth was the salvation of sinners (Matt. 1:21, Luke 2:11).

As in the first two Gospels, John the Baptist, the baptism and the temptation are also dealt with by Luke. These inaugurate the ministry of Jesus. In the ministry of John, Jesus is linked with the

Old Testament messianic prophecies. In His baptism, Jesus identifies Himself with the people that He has come to save (3:21), and in the temptations He has His first confrontation with, and triumphs over, the terrible enemy of souls.

Obviously, much is included in Luke with which Matthew and Mark have also dealt, but Luke also provides important material peculiar to his Gospel. There are 18 parables that are found only in this Gospel (see the list of parables). Luke alone tells us of the Good Samaritan (10:31); of the tax-collector (18:13); of the Prodigal Son (15:11–20); of Zacchaeus (19:2). It is only in Luke that we read that Jesus wept over Jerusalem (19:41); of the sweat like drops of blood in Gethsemane (22:42); of the conversion of the thief on the cross (23:43); of the two on the road to Emmaus (24:13). Luke records for us more prayers of Jesus than the other Gospel writers. In fact, Luke thoroughly fulfils his stated aim (1:3) to discover the facts and to write a full account of the life and ministry of the Lord Jesus Christ. Unlike Matthew and Mark, Luke begins his account of the ministry in Galilee (4:14–9:50) with the story of the rejection of Jesus at Nazareth, and he gives more space to it than his fellow Gospel writers. 'Although we do not know why Luke places the rejection at Nazareth so early, the suggestion that he may have done this in order to indicate at once what would be the general trend with respect to the people's attitude to Jesus deserves consideration. That trend would be: first enthusiastic interest and amazement, then rejection' (William Hendriksen).

The amazement of the people as they heard the teaching of Jesus is recorded time and time again by Luke – 4:32, 36; 5:26; 7:16. The crowds flocked to Him to hear the Word of God (5:1). We must never forget that the Lord Jesus Christ was a preacher. He Himself saw preaching as crucial to His fulfilling the will of God. He said, 'I must preach the good news . . . because that is why I was sent' (4:43). 'It is fashionable in some circles, to play down the importance of preaching in the church. It is claimed that the Gospel is conveyed much less effectively by what we say, than by what we do and what we are. There is no avoiding the fact, however, that in these opening scenes of the ministry of Jesus the way God's messsage "comes across" is by words: one man speaks, other men hear' (Michael Wilcock).

Preaching and miracle-working characterized the ministry of

Jesus in Galilee. The response to this varied from the amazing faith of the centurion (7:9) to the equally amazing hatred of the Pharisees (6:11).

The journey to Jerusalem (9:51–19:27) contains most of the parables and other material that only Luke records for us. The main content of this section is the teaching of Jesus and here we have 20 of Luke's 28 parables. 'This is in many respects the most important part of the third Gospel because the major portion of its contents does not occur in the three other Gospels. In addition, we find in these chapters many of the most beautiful parables of the Saviour – e.g. that of the good Samaritan, the prodigal son, the lost sheep, the lost coin, and so on. If these priceless parables of the Saviour had not been recorded in Luke, they would have been lost to us forever, for the majority of them are not recorded in the other Gospels' (Norval Geldenhuys).

Jesus knew he was going to die in Jerusalem, as is indicated in 9:51, 'He steadfastly set His face to go to Jerusalem' (AV). With death so near, perhaps this is why there is so much teaching in this section as Jesus prepares His disciples for their ministry of preaching the Gospel after He has left them. This task would be no easy one, as indicated in 10:3, 'I am sending you out like lambs among wolves'. The truth of this statement is very evident in Acts, but the encouragement is the promised aid of the Holy Spirit (12:12). In the same passage, we find teaching on concern for others (10:30–37); prayer (11:1–13); trust (12:22–34); watchfulness (12:35–48); and the cost of discipleship (14:25–35) – all crucial lessons for those who seek to spread the gospel.

The last section (19:28–24:53) deals with the events of the last week and the resurrection. Like the other three Gospels, Luke commences his account with the triumphal entry and tells us that the crowd shouted, 'Blessed is the King who comes in the name of the Lord'. This is a quotation from Psalm 118:26. They were clearly acknowledging Jesus to be the Messiah, but none of them realised what exactly the Messiah had to do. The cross was only a few days away. The shouts of acclamation on Palm Sunday were to be followed by "Crucify him!" on Good Friday. It is often said that the passage shows how fickle the crowd was to change their cry in a few days. But how true is this? Luke tells us that the Palm Sunday crowd were disciples of Jesus (19:37) – probably pilgrims from Galilee, down in Jerusalem for the Passover. The crowd who shouted 'Crucify him' in chapter 20:21, were doing so in the very early hours of Friday morning and were probably hand picked by the Pharisees for the arrest and trials of Jesus. They were two entirely different crowds.

Even though Jesus had sought to prepare the disciples for His betrayal and death, when it happened they were completely shattered. Peter disowned Jesus (22:54-62), the women mourned and wailed (23:77), and the whole problem was high-lighted by Cleopas and his friend on the road to Emmaus (24:13-35). They had heard about the resurrection (vv.22-24) but they did not believe it. Consequently, they were still downcast (v.17). Jesus, whom at this point they did not recognize, very gently but firmly rebuked them (vv.25-27). He showed them from the Old Testament Scriptures that what had happened was in full accord with the plan and purpose of God. And note v.32. Their gloom was lifted and their hearts began to burn with hope, not only when they finally recognized Jesus but when the scriptures were opened to them.

STUDY MATERIAL

Expository thoughts on the Gospels – Luke by J. C. Ryle (Banner of Truth, 1986).
The Message of Luke in *The Bible Speaks Today* series by Michael Wilcock (Inter-Varsity Press, 1979).

∽ 5 ∽

John

The fourth Gospel was written much later than the other three, probably about AD 90, and tradition tells us that it was written by the Apostle John. As well as tradition there is very strong evidence in the Gospel itself that the writer was indeed John. The author was an eye-witness of the life of Jesus (1:14). Coupled with this is the strange fact that neither John nor his brother James are mentioned by name in this Gospel. Such a glaring omission only makes sense if one of these two men was the author and 'felt a natural delicacy about introducing his own and his brother's name into a narrative of the Lord's life' (Gresham Machen). So which of the two brothers is it? We must say John, on the basis of the fact that James was martyred about AD 44 (Acts 12:2). The early church had no doubt about John's authorship and taught that he wrote this Gospel towards the end of his life, whilst at Ephesus.

By the time John was written, the other three Gospels had been circulating for over twenty years. From Matthew, Mark and Luke the believers knew the facts about the life of Jesus, so John is not interested in merely repeating all these. He omits much (20:30). Among the incidents omitted are those of Jesus's baptism and the institution by Jesus of the Lord's Supper as a permanent remembrance of his death.

The purpose of the Gospel of John is to encourage faith in Jesus Christ, the Son of God (20:31).

'The theme of John's Gospel is the Deity of the Saviour. Here, as nowhere else in Scripture so fully, the Godhood of Christ is presented to our view. That which is outstanding in this fourth Gospel is the Divine Sonship of the Lord Jesus. In this book we are shown that the One who walked this earth for thirty-three years, who was crucified at Calvary, who rose in triumph from the grave, and who forty days later departed from these scenes, was none other than the Lord of Glory. The evidence for this is overwhelming, the proofs almost without number, and the effect of contemplating them must be to bow our hearts in worship before "the great God and our Saviour Jesus Christ" (Titus 2:13)' (Arthur W. Pink).

John is quite different from the other three Gospels. Here there is no account of: the birth of Jesus; the temptation; the transfiguration; and there are no parables. John shows us instead the personal and intimate ministry of Jesus to people like Nicodemus, the Samaritan woman, and the apostles (chapters 13–17). Here, too, we have the most marvellous declarations of the deity of Jesus in the 'I ams':

I AM the bread of life	6:35
I AM the light of the world	8:12
Before Abraham was born I AM	8:58
I AM the gate	10:7
I AM the Good Shepherd	10:11
I AM the resurrection and the life	11:25
I AM the way and the truth and the life	14:6
I AM the true vine	15:1

Charles Hodge commenting on John 8:58 said that Jesus was 'thereby asserting not only His pre-existence, but His eternity, as He declares Himself to be the "I AM", that is, the self-existing and immutable Jehovah'.

CONTENTS

SUMMARY

The prologue in the opening eighteen verses is a magnificent statement as to who Jesus is. 'The prologue provides at the very start the heavenly point of view from which the whole of the Gospel history must be contemplated. Verse 14, especially, strikes the key note of the book. The Fourth Gospel is intended to exhibit the glory of the incarnate Son of God. It exhibits it not merely by the adulation of a disciple, not merely by the rehearsing of Christian experience, but by simple testimony to what actually occurred on earth. The testimony of an eyewitness to the glory of the incarnate Word – that forms the content of this book' (J. Gresham Machen).

The statement about Jesus being the incarnate Word (1:14) is further strengthened by the declaration of John the Baptist that He is the Lamb of God who takes away the sin of the world (1:29). In chapter two the power and authority of Jesus are underlined in the first miracle and the cleansing of the temple.

Thus, at the very beginning, John sets before us the uniqueness of Jesus. The miracles were signs to show us who Jesus is. They are not ends in themselves but are intended to lead to faith, as is evident in 2:11. The cleansing of the temple was also a confirmation to the disciples of the uniqueness of Jesus. They saw it as a fulfilment of Psalm 69:9 (v.17).

Two long discourses in chapters 3 and 4 show us Jesus dealing with people at the extreme ends of the social strata of the day. In the sight of God, however, the ultra-respectable Nicodemus and the immoral Samaritan woman are both sinners who need what only Jesus can provide. The same is true of the man healed at the Pool of Bethesda in chapter 5. He must 'stop sinning or something worse may happen' to him (v.14).

In chapter six we have a long section on the bread of life. This took place near the time of the Passover (v.4) and was exactly a year before the cross. Christ's words were spoken in Capernaum (v.59) amongst people who for two years had seen and heard Him more than any others. Their initial reaction to the feeding of the five thousand was one of enthusiasm and they were willing to risk their lives in an uprising against the Romans to make Jesus king (v.15). But Jesus is not impressed (v.26) and now begins to teach them doctrine (vv.32–59). It is their response to this teaching that really shows their real feelings towards Jesus and sadly they reject Him (vv.60, 66). The popular adoration of Jesus is over and the Pharisees intensify their plans to kill Him (7:1). What they do not realize is that the time He will die is not to be set by them but by God (7:30).

The opposition to Jesus grows and earns the strong rebuke from Jesus that 'you belong to your father the devil' (8:44). The spiritual blindness of these people is incredible. The clear evidence in chapter 9 of a man born blind now being able to see because Jesus had healed him is rejected. 'They were determined not to believe. They were resolved that no evidence should change their minds, and no proofs influence their will. They were like men who shut their eyes and tie a bandage over them, and refuse to have it untied' (J. C. Ryle).

The picture in chapter 10 of Jesus as the Good Shepherd is one of the most beautiful in the New Testament. The shepherd picture is also used widely in the Old Testament (Psa. 23; 78:52; 80:1). 'Jesus is identifying Himself with the Shepherd of Old Testament Scripture – "I am the good Shepherd". To the Jewish person that meant only one thing; it meant God. There was only One good, there was only one Shepherd, there was only One who had the right to the title "The Good Shepherd". Here is someone they knew, someone who was brought up amongst them, and He stands out in front of them and says, "I am the Good Shepherd". If you go down to the thirty-third verse in that chapter, you will find that they charge Him with blasphemy. Why? Because He made Himself equal with God. You see, that is what His claim was – "I am the Good Shepherd". It was a claim to full and absolute deity, to identify with the One they knew as the Good Shepherd' (J. Douglas Macmillan).

If chapter 10 contains a claim to deity, chapter 11 supplies abundant proof that the claim is not fraudulent, as divine power is unleashed to raise Lazarus from the grave. Even this does not convince some that Jesus is the Christ. Though they acknowledge the validity of the miracle (11:47), they still plot to kill Him. So Jesus withdraws from public life for a while (11:54).

The last week of Jesus's life starts in John 12 with the triumphal entry into Jerusalem. This is in total contrast to the withdrawal of 11:54 and shows that Jesus is taking the initiative. Though the Pharisees wanted to kill the Saviour, they would not have done it at the Passover. By the very nature of His entry into Jerusalem, Jesus was forcing their hand. Passover was God's appointed time for Him to die as the Lamb of God who takes away our sin. Paul said in 1 Corinthians 5:7, 'For Christ, our Passover Lamb, has been sacrificed'.

Chapters 13–17 show us Jesus alone with the apostles on the Thursday evening before Calvary. This is the last time before His death that He will be with these men and He uses the time to set them an example on service (13:1–17); to comfort them (14:1–14); to promise them the Holy Spirit (14:15–31); and, above all, to pray for them (17:1–26).

The remaining chapters deal with the arrest, trial, death and resurrection of Jesus.

William Hendriksen described the Gospel of John as 'the most amazing book that was ever written'. No Christian would argue with that. We might add that the four Gospels together are a thing of beauty unsurpassed in all literature.

'Thus end these peerless Histories – this Fourfold Gospel. And who that has walked with us through this Garden of the Lord, these "beds of spices", has not often said, with Peter on the mount of transfiguration, It is good to be here! Who that has reverentially and lovingly bent over the sacred text has not found himself in the presence of the Word made flesh – has not beheld the glory of the Only-begotten of the Father, full of grace and truth – has not felt His warm, tender hand upon him, and heard that voice saying to himself, as so often to the disciples of old, "Fear not!" Well, dear reader, "Abide in Him", and let "His words" – as here recorded – "abide in thee"' (David Brown).

STUDY MATERIAL

Expository thoughts on the Gospels – John by J. C. Ryle (Banner of Truth, 1987).
Jesus and His Friends (John 14–17) by D. A. Carson (Inter-Varsity Press, 1986).

∽ 6 ∽

The Last Week

We have seen how much space the four Gospels give to the events of the last week of Jesus's life from Palm Sunday to Easter Sunday. From all the Gospels we can build up a complete picture of that crucial week.

SUNDAY	Triumphal entry
	Visit to the temple
	Return to Bethany
MONDAY	The cursing of the barren fig tree
	The cleansing of the temple
	Return to Bethany
TUESDAY	This was the last day of public teaching
	Parables: The two sons
	The wicked husbandmen
	The marriage of the king's son
	The ten virgins
	The talents
	Questions from the Sadducees on resurrection and from the Pharisees on the great command
	Jesus denounces the Scribes and Pharisees
	The lamentation over Jerusalem
	The widow's mite
	Prophecy of the overthrow of the temple and the second coming
	The last judgement
WEDNESDAY	Nothing recorded in Scripture
THURSDAY	The last supper

Gethsemane
The betrayal
The arrest

FRIDAY   Late Thursday night and in the early hours of Friday:
Jesus before Annas, Caiaphas, the Sanhedrin
The denials by Peter
Jesus condemned by the Sanhedrin for blasphemy
About 6 a.m. The Roman trial
                 Jesus before Pilate and then Herod
      9 a.m. Jesus is led away to Calvary
      3 p.m. Jesus dies
              Veil rent
              Earthquake
              The burial

SATURDAY   Jesus in the grave
SUNDAY   The resurrection

৩৬ 7 ৩৬

The Gospel in the Gospels

Matthew, Mark, Luke and John were men with a message, and this message has at its centre and heart the cross of the Lord Jesus Christ. This is why they all give so much space to the events from Palm Sunday to Easter Sunday. Without the resurrection, the life and ministry of Jesus would have been for them a complete failure. All the hopes of the apostles would have been dashed to the ground. They would have concluded either that Jesus had misled them or that they themselves had placed too much expectation on one man. They obviously felt this temptation in the hours from Friday to Sunday morning, and even when they heard of the resurrection, none of them believed it at first. Thomas was not the only apostle to doubt! But the resurrection changed everything. It enabled them to understand the true purpose of the Messiah because it showed them the glory of the cross. Consequently, when they write their Gospels years later, they do so in the light of the great and glorious gospel of the cross and resurrection of Christ. So in the four Gospels, the gospel shines out in all its essential elements, which we will now summarize.

The Fact of Sin

The good news of the gospel is set against the dark background of man in sin. The accounts of Christ's birth in both Matthew and Luke make it clear that He has come to save men from their sin (Matt. 1:21, Luke 2:11). It is the fact of sin that makes the gospel necessary. The message of John the Baptist makes this very clear. He accused the Pharisees and Sadducees of being a brood of vipers (Matt. 3:7). Jesus continues this theme and at the beginning of His preaching He quotes Isaiah, and declares that His ministry is to be to those living in darkness and in the land of the shadow of death (Matt. 4:16). This includes not only the Pharisees and Sadducees but all men and women. Jesus sent His disciples to 'the lost sheep of Israel' (Matt. 10:6). They were lost; they were 'a wicked and adulterous generation' (Matt. 12:39) and 'their heart has become callous' (Matt. 13:15).

Our tendency is to see the sin of someone else but not our own. Jesus warned about this in the Sermon on the Mount (Matt. 7:1-5) and also in Luke 13:1-5.

The Reality of Judgement and Hell

Just as sin is real, so too is God's wrath and condemnation. 'Repent or perish' is the terrible challenge of the gospel. Many of the parables in Luke teach clearly that not only does sin deserve punishment but it will certainly receive punishment unless it is dealt with.

The rich man and Lazarus (Luke 16:19-31) brings home the terrible reality of hell. The parable of the tenants (Luke 20:9-18) shows that no-one will escape the consequence of his sin, and ends with the evil-doers being dealt with. The rich fool (Luke 12:16-21) warns us that judgement may come sooner than we think.

No-one can read the Gospels without seeing the terrible reality of hell. In Matthew 25:41 we read Christ's statement which many are to hear in the future: 'Depart from me, you who are cursed, into eternal fire prepared for the devil and his angels'. These words cannot but show us how seriously God regards sin. The impenitent and the unbelieving 'will go away into eternal punishment' (Matt. 25:44).

All four Gospels deal with this awful subject. 'John makes it quite clear that unless sin is dealt with men will perish eternally. The giving of the only-begotten Son preserves believers from this, but the plain implication of John 3:16 is that those who do not believe do not have everlasting life. They "perish". The text is usually cited to show God's love and the wonder of the provision He has made for man's salvation in Christ, but it should not be overlooked that the love of which it speaks is directed towards saving men from a dire fate, not play-acting in a situation where there is no real peril. For John the possibility of perishing is a very real one indeed. And his reference to "the world" shows that this is no restricted thing. All men stand in danger' (Leon Morris).

The Atonement

The only answer to human sin and divine wrath is God's answer. God sent Jesus to bear our sin and guilt and to face the divine wrath instead of us. Jesus came 'to give his life as a ransom for many' (Mark 10:45), to deal with our sin (John 1:29) and to lay down His life for us (John 15:13).

The doctrine of the atonement is the biblical teaching on what the death of the Lord Jesus Christ means. The Gospel writers see it in terms of Jesus coming into the world for the particular purpose of giving His life as a ransom for many.

'In the ancient world the "ransom" was the price paid for release. It applied widely to the release of prisoners of war or slaves. The Old Testament adds another use. In certain circumstances a man under sentence of death might be released on payment of a ransom (Exodus 21:30). Apart from metaphorical passages, these three groupings give us the uniform usage in antiquity. There is always a plight into which a man has fallen, be it captivity or slavery or condemnation. There is always the payment of the price which effects release, and it is this price that is called the "ransom".

'Each of the above situations has point in the Christian scheme. Like the prisoner of war, man is in the power of the enemy. Christ has paid the ransom, freeing him and bringing him back where he belongs. The sinner is a slave. He is in bondage to his sins. Christ has paid the price, his life, which brings relief to the sinner. As a result he is a free man. The sinner is under sentence of death on account of his sin. His life is forfeit. But the forfeited lives of many are liberated by the surrender of Christ's life' (Leon Morris).

Jesus deals with our sin by taking it away from us. He takes it to the cross, where it is justly punished by God. There are only two places where God deals finally with sin. One is in hell, where it is eternally punished and the other is at Calvary, where Jesus was punished instead of the sinner and consequently where the sinner can be forgiven. Thus, Jesus is seen as our substitute. He is the

innocent Lamb who dies instead of the guilty sinner. See John 15:13
and also John 11:50 with 18:14. So Jesus quite deliberately goes to
the cross to die. 'The Good Shepherd lays down His life for the
sheep' (John 10:11). This He does at the command of the Father
(John 10:18) and if He had not deliberately laid down His life, no-
one could have taken it from Him. All this means that Jesus is the
only Saviour (John 14:6). He is God's answer to human sin.

> The holy law fulfilled,
> Atonement now is made,
> And our great debt, too great for us,
> He now has fully paid.
>
> For in His death our death
> Died with Him on the tree,
> And a great number by His blood
> Will go to heaven made free.
>
> *John Elias*

The Necessity of Repentance and Faith

The response that God requires from sinners to what Jesus has done
is repentance and faith. Hence we find Jesus preaching repentance
(Mark 1:15). Repentance has two sides: it is a turning from sin and
to God. For true repentance both these elements are essential. A
man can turn from sins without turning to God. He may see the
value of 'turning over a new leaf' and decide to refrain from certain
bad habits. No doubt this will do him good in a variety of ways, but
spiritually it will be useless. On the other hand, a man may turn to
God and cry for mercy, but have no intention of leaving his sin. His
eyes may be wet with tears while his heart is as hard as stone.

Faith is believing who Jesus is and what He has done for us.
Where there is true faith, there will inevitably be repentance. 'Faith
is not itself a meritorious act. It is not a way of earning salvation. It is
a way of receiving a gift' (J. Gresham Machen).

A lovely picture of repentance and faith is seen in the parable of
the prodigal son (Luke 15:11–32). Man in sin is vividly set out in
verses 11–17. Then the prodigal comes to his senses (v.18) – that is,
he begins to think for the first time of his plight and of the love of the

father. He acknowledges his sin and guilt (vv.18–19), and knows
that he is totally unworthy. Here is repentance, but there is also
faith in the goodness of the father. It is a faith that is well founded
as verses 22–24 reveal.

The Blessing of Forgiveness

The death of Jesus secures for the repentant sinner forgiveness of
sin. Jesus said at the Lord's Supper, 'This is my blood of the new
covenant, which is poured out for many for the forgiveness of sins'
(Matt. 26:28).

'Another detail peculiar to Luke's Gospel is Jesus' prayer for
those who crucified Him, "Father, forgive them; for they know not
what they do" (Luke 23:34). This word of the dying Saviour is not
out of line with Luke's interests. He has a great deal to say about
forgiveness throughout his Gospel. In addition to this prayer, he
records the prayer that Christ taught His followers to pray,
wherein they seek forgiveness (Luke 11:4); he tells us of occasions
when men were forgiven (Luke 5:20, 24; 7:47), he includes the
charge that "repentance and remission of sins" should be preached
throughout the world (Luke 24:47), and he looks through to the
last day and speaks of what will and what will not be forgiven then
(Luke 12:10). Now if men need forgiveness, then clearly their own
way is not good enough. And the place Luke gives forgiveness
shows the importance he attaches to it' (Leon Morris).

The Grace of God

All the truths and blessings of the gospel rest upon the foundation
of the unmerited and unsought grace of God. Salvation is all of
God. No-one deserves to be saved, and such is the hold that sin has
on human nature that, left to ourselves, none of us would even
want to be saved. 'Men do not think of themselves as sinners and
therefore they see no need of a Saviour. It requires a divine work
within them before they can see themselves as they really are
before God. Only as the Spirit of God works within them do they
become convicted' (Leon Morris).

John deals with this divine work more especially in chapters 3 and 6. Nicodemus, although he was a very religious man, needed to be born again. Why? Because he was by nature, like all men and women, spiritually dead. This new birth or regeneration is the exclusive work of God the Holy Spirit (3:8). Unless this work of grace takes place, we cannot be saved, because 'No one can come to me,' said Jesus, 'unless the Father who sent me draws him' (John 6:44). In John 6:37–44 we see very clearly man's inability to convert himself. He must be drawn by God. It is the essential work of God that creates conviction of sin, faith and repentance.

'Men are not saved because they turn over a new leaf. Conversion is not a meritorious action which ought to be suitably rewarded. Conversion, as the New Testament understands it, means a wholehearted turning away from sin. It means a ceasing to rely on one's own strong right arm. It means a coming to rely entirely on the mercy of God. Apart from that mercy conversion would be aimless, futile, meaningless. Conversion roots salvation squarely in the action of God, and it takes its meaning from the action of God' (Leon Morris).

Eternal Life

The salvation that God gives to His people is not something belonging only to this life, it is eternal. To be saved means to cross from death to life (John 5:24), and the life is eternal life. The grave is no hindrance to this (John 5:28–29) because Jesus has conquered death and the grave. Christ's triumph becomes ours. 'An interesting group of passages extends the ultimate triumph to the followers of Jesus. They will have a share in resurrection itself (Luke 20:35, 37). Associated with this is the heavenly reward of those who follow Christ, that reward which is "great in heaven" (Luke 6:23). So important is this whole idea that it is no gain if a man could acquire the whole world and in the process lose his soul (Luke 9:25)' (Leon Morris).

Jesus shows us clearly that eternal life means eternal security. We can never lose our salvation (John 10:28–29). To have eternal life means that we can never perish. 'For God so loved the world that he gave his only begotten Son, that whoever believes in him shall not perish but have eternal life' (John 3:16). 'Everlasting life is of course ever-during happiness. The happiness of a being like man, consists in the Divine favour, and image, and fellowship; in knowing God, in loving God, in being loved by God, in knowing that we are loved by God; in venerating God, trusting in God; having our mind conformed to his mind, our wishes subjected to his pleasure, thinking along with him, willing along with him, choosing what he chooses, seeking and finding enjoyment in what he finds enjoyment. This is life. This is happiness. And the never-ending continuance of this is eternal life. To obtain this kind of happiness for men, for men of every nation under heaven, and to secure the permanent enjoyment of it during the whole eternity of their being, – this is the great and glorious object of the divinely commissioned God-man, the Messiah' (John Brown).

New Testament Parables

	Matthew	Mark	Luke
Salt	5:13		14:34–35
Light	5:14–15	4:21–22	8:16
Two builders	7:24–27		6:47–49
Garments and wine-skins	9:16–17	2:21–22	5:36–38
Sower	13:3–8	4:3–8	8:5–8
Weeds	13:24–30		
Mustard seed	13:31–32	4:30–32	13:18–19
Yeast	13:33		13:20–21
Treasure hidden in a field	13:44		
Fine pearls	13:45–46		
Net full of fish	13:47–48		
Lost sheep	18:10–14		15:4–7
Unmerciful servant	18:23–34		
Workers in the vine-yard	20:1–16		
Two sons	21:28–32		
Tenants	21:33–46	12:1–12	20:9–19
Wedding banquet	22:1–14		
Fig tree	24:32–35	13:28–31	21:29–33

Ten virgins	25:1–13		
Talents	25:14–30		
Sheep and goats	25:31–46		
Growing seed		4:26–29	
Two debtors			7:41–43
Good Samaritan			10:25–37
Friend at midnight			11:5–8
Rich fool			12:13–21
Watchfulness			12:35–41
Wise manager			12:42–48
Barren fig tree			13:6–9
Wedding feast			14:7–14
Great banquet			14:15–24
Counting the cost			14:28–33
Lost coin			15:8–10
Lost son			15:11–32
Shrewd manager			16:1–9
Rich man and Lazarus			16:19–31
Farmer and servant			17:7–10
Persistent widow			18:1–8
Pharisee and the tax collector			18:9–14
Ten minas (pounds)			19:11–27

New Testament Miracles

	Matthew	Mark	Luke	John
Leper	8:1–4	1:40–45	5:12–15	
Centurion's servant	8:5–13		7:1–10	
Peter's mother-in-law	8:14–15	1:30–31	4:38–39	
Stilling the storm	8:23–27	4:35–41	8:22–25	
Legion	8:28–34	5:1–15	8:27–35	
Paralytic	9:1–8	2:1–12	5:17–26	
Jairus' daughter	9:18–26	5:21–43	8:41–56	
Woman with haemorrhage	9:20–22	5:25–29	8:43–48	
Two blind men	9:27–31			

Demon-possessed man	9:32–33		
Man with the shrivel-led hand	12:9–13	3:1–5	6:6–11
Blind and dumb man	12:22		11:14
Feeding of 5000	14:15–21	6:35–44	9:12–17	6:5–14
Walking on water	14:25	6:48–51		6:19–21
Canaanite woman's daughter	15:21–28	7:24–30	
Feeding of 4000	15:32–39	8:1–9	
Epileptic boy	17:14–21	9:14–29	9:37–42
Coin in fish's mouth	17:24–27		
Bartimaeus	20:29–34	10:46–52	18:35–43
The fig tree withers	21:17–22	11:12–14 11:20–26	
Drives out an evil spirit		1:23–26	4:33–36
Deaf and dumb man		7:31–37	
Blind man at Bethsa-ida		8:22–26	
Catch of fish			5:1–11
Widow of Nain's son			7:11–16
Crippled woman			13:10–17
Man with dropsy			14:1–6
Ten lepers			17:11–19
Malchus' ear			22:49–51
Water to wine				2:1–11
Boy at Capernaum				4:46–54
Pool of Bethesda				5:1–16
Man born blind				9:1–8
Lazarus				11:1–45
Another catch of fish				21:1–14

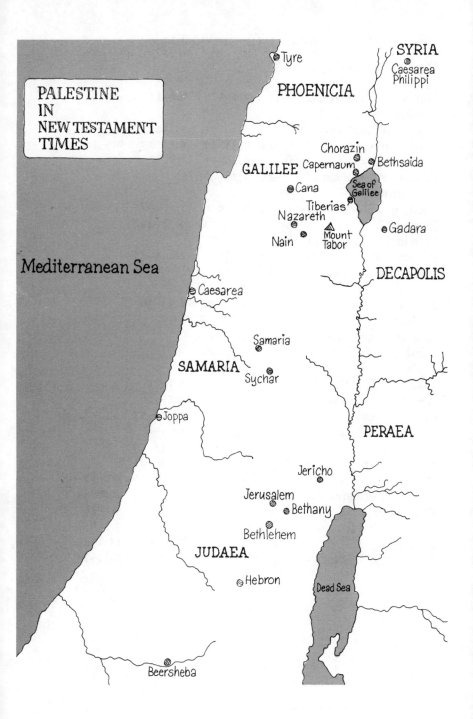

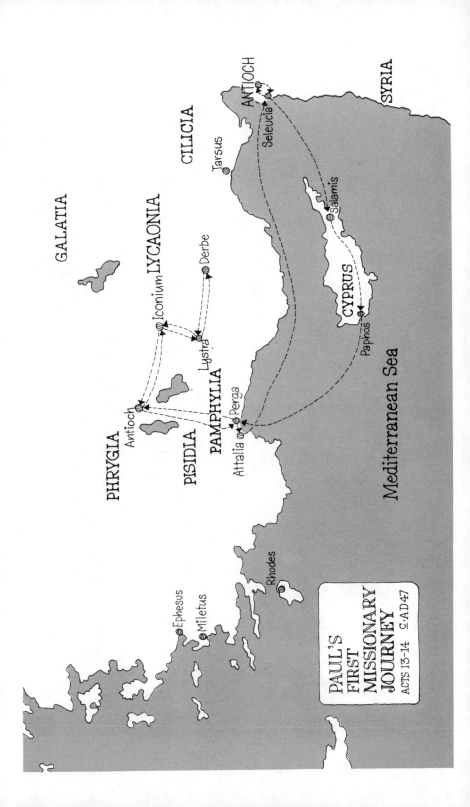

GALATIA

PHRYGIA

PISIDIA

PAMPHYLIA

LYCAONIA

CILICIA

SYRIA

ANTIOCH

Seleucia

Tarsus

Iconium

Derbe

Lystra

Antioch

Perga

Attalia

Salamis

CYPRUS

Paphos

Rhodes

Ephesus

Miletus

Mediterranean Sea

PAUL'S
FIRST
MISSIONARY
JOURNEY
ACTS 13-14 C·AD47

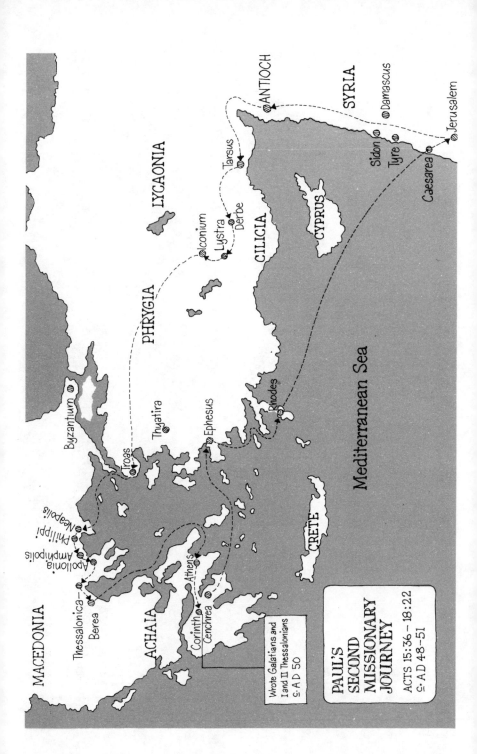

MACEDONIA

Thessalonica
Berea

Neapolis
Philippi
Apollonia
Amphipolis

ACHAIA

Athens
Corinth
Cenchrea

Byzantium

Thyatira

Troas

Ephesus

Rhodes

CRETE

PHRYGIA

LYCAONIA

Iconium
Lystra
Derbe

CILICIA

Tarsus

ANTIOCH

CYPRUS

Mediterranean Sea

SYRIA

Damascus

Sidon
Tyre

Caesarea

Jerusalem

Wrote Galatians and
I and II Thessalonians
c. A.D. 50

PAUL'S
SECOND
MISSIONARY
JOURNEY

ACTS 15:36 – 18:22
c. A.D. 48–51

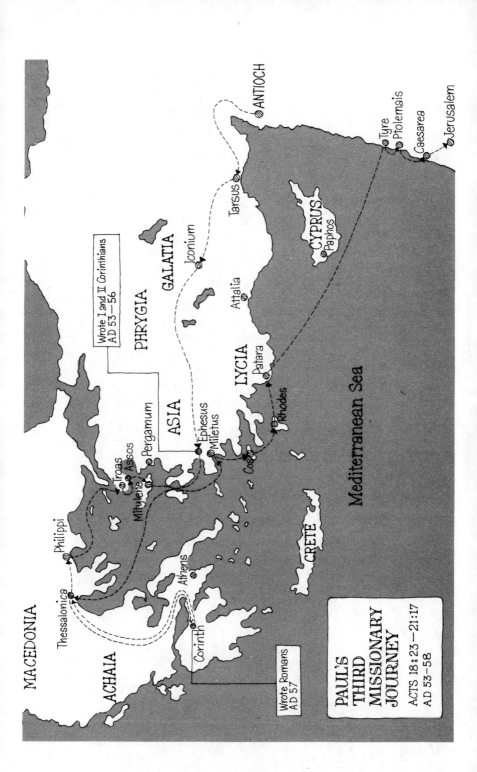

MACEDONIA

ACHAIA

Thessalonica

Philippi

Athens

Corinth

Wrote Romans
AD 57

PAUL'S
THIRD
MISSIONARY
JOURNEY

ACTS 18:23—21:17

AD 53—58

Troas
Assos
Mitylene

Pergamum

ASIA

Ephesus
Miletus

PHRYGIA

GALATIA

Wrote I and II Corinthians
AD 53—56

Iconium

Tarsus

ANTIOCH

CYPRUS
Paphos

Tyre
Ptolemais
Caesarea
Jerusalem

Attalia

LYCIA

Patara

Rhodes

Cos

CRETE

Mediterranean Sea

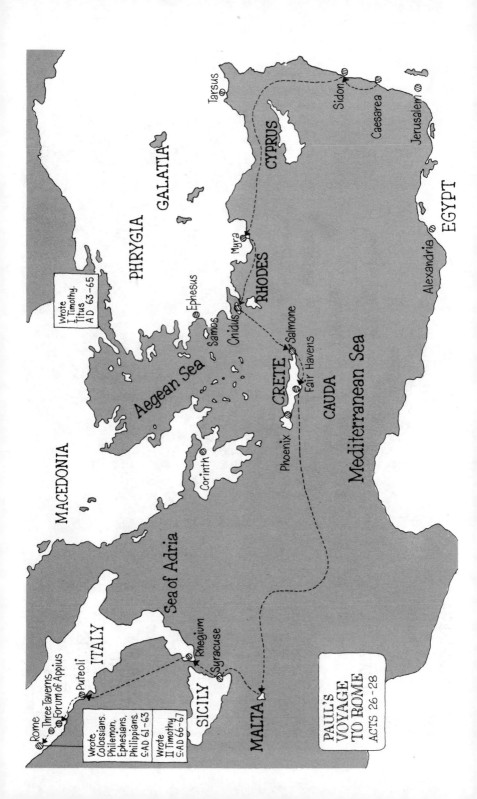

MACEDONIA

ITALY

Rome
Three Taverns
Forum of Appius
Puteoli

Sea of Adria

Rhegium
Syracuse

SICILY

MALTA

Wrote Colossians,
Philemon,
Ephesians,
Philippians,
c.AD 61–63

Wrote II Timothy
c.AD 66–67

PAUL'S
VOYAGE
TO ROME
ACTS 26–28

Corinth

Phoenix

CRETE

Fair Havens

CAUDA

Salmone

Cnidus

Samos

Ephesus

Aegean Sea

PHRYGIA

GALATIA

Wrote
I Timothy,
Titus
AD 63–65

Myra

RHODES

CYPRUS

Mediterranean Sea

Tarsus

Sidon

Caesarea

Jerusalem

Alexandria

EGYPT

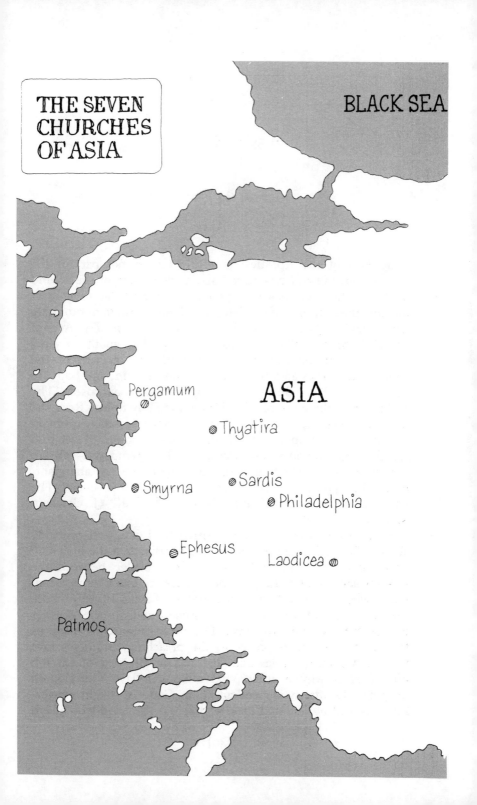

ஒ 8 ஒ

Acts

'The Acts of the Apostles' is a title that is not part of the
original writing and was added about the middle of the second
century. The book makes no pretence to record the ministry of
all the apostles, only two, Peter and Paul. A more appropriate
title would be 'The Acts of Jesus Christ' (1:1) or 'The Acts of
the Holy Spirit'. The book covers a period of about 30 years
and is a thrilling account of the birth and growth of the
Church. Blessings and problems go hand in hand, and both are
used by the Holy Spirit to accomplish God's purposes. 'The
real actor in the book of The Acts is the Holy Spirit. Read the
book all together, or read it in great stretches, and you obtain
an irresistible impression of the Spirit's power. Jews and
Gentiles, rulers and kings, the sea and its tempests – all are
powerless before the march of the gospel. Joyous, abundant,
irresistible power – that is the keynote of the book. The
triumphant progress of the Church of God!' (J. Gresham
Machen).

As we have seen, Acts was written by Luke, and probably
about AD 65. The book is of great importance in the historical
framework of Scripture because it is a bridge between the
Gospels and Paul's writings. The epistles are much more mean-
ingful when we read them in the context of Acts. In Acts we see
the founding of the various churches and in the epistles
we see the life and problems. The book pulsates with life as
the Holy Spirit gives power to the preaching, promotes love
for the brethren, guides and instructs in all areas of Church
life. This is why it is so vital a book today. The Church
in Acts was utterly dependent upon God. It sought prayerfully the will of God and inevitably it was the Lord who added

to the Church such as should be saved. The determination to obey Jesus and spread the gospel world-wide is a lesson for us.

All this does not mean that the Church in Acts was perfect and free from quarrels. There were jealousies (Acts 6) and leaders had differences of opinion that got very sharp and contentious (Acts 15). But these were not allowed to dominate the scene or cloud the main issue and mar the work. The Church in Acts was not perfect but it was powerful. It was not without its faults but it was faithful.

Perhaps a word of caution needs to be sounded concerning some of the actions of the young churches in Acts. We are to take our pattern for the Christian life from the teaching of Scripture, not from all the actions of the characters recorded in Scripture. For instance, the selling of possessions in Acts 2:44, 45 and 4:32 was done with the highest motives, but is that to be the pattern of how we are to conduct our lives? The New Testament has much to say about the giving of money to maintain the Church and to help those less fortunate than ourselves, but we are never commanded to sell all our possessions and share everything. The selflessness behind the action is to be copied by us because it is commanded throughout Scripture, but the particular actions are not obligatory, because they are not commanded.

'The book before us is a special history of the planting and extension of the church, both among Jews and Gentiles, by the gradual establishment of radiating centres or sources of influence at certain salient points throughout a large part of the empire, beginning at Jerusalem and ending at Rome. That this is really the theme and purpose of the history, any reader may satisfy himself by running through it with this general idea in his mind, observing how the prominent points answer to it, and that as soon as this idea is exhausted the book closes, in a way that would be otherwise abrupt and harsh' (J. A. Alexander).

CONTENTS

9:1–31	Paul's conversion
9:32–12:25	Peter's ministry
13–14	Paul's first missionary journey
15:1–35	The Council at Jerusalem
15:36–18:22	Paul's second missionary journey
18:23–21:16	Paul's third missionary journey
21:17–23:30	Paul at Jerusalem
23:31–26:32	Paul at Caesarea
27:1–28:14	Journey to Rome
28:15–31	Paul at Rome

It will be helpful also to see the contents of Acts in relationship to the period of 30 years covered by the book. The dates are to be regarded as approximate but accurate to within one or two years:

AD 30	The birth of the Church	Acts 1–2
AD 34	Paul's conversion	Acts 9
AD 46–47	Paul's first missionary journey	Acts 13–14
AD 48	Council at Jerusalem	Acts 15
AD 48–51	Paul's second missionary journey	Acts 15:36–18:22
AD 53	Start of Paul's third missionary journey	Acts 18:23
AD 54–57	Paul's ministry at Ephesus	Acts 19
AD 57–58	Paul in Greece	Acts 20
AD 58	Back to Jerusalem	Acts 21
AD 58–60	In prison at Caesarea	Acts 24–26
AD 60–61	Paul's voyage to Rome	Acts 27–28

SUMMARY

As we have seen, Acts is a history of the planting and extension of the Church, but how was this achieved? As you read Acts, the answer becomes very clear. The planting and extension was done by the preaching of the Word of God in the power of the Holy Spirit. So the book can be seen basically as the record of the ministry of two preachers, Peter in the first twelve chapters and Paul in the remaining chapters. Obviously there is some overlapping but it is the preaching of these two men that dominates Acts. As well as these two great men, the whole Church is also involved in spreading the gospel (Acts 8:4).

[42]

The book opens with the Christians still not clear as to the worldwide purpose and extent of the gospel. Just before the ascension they ask Jesus, 'Lord, are you at this time going to restore the kingdom to Israel?' (1:6). These men were Jews and they still thought in the old Jewish way of the exclusiveness of the Jewish people in receiving God's blessing. This misconception was to surface on many occasions in the early Church and cause serious problems (see Acts 10:9–23; 11:19; 15:1). The Lord's answer to the question was that when the power of the Holy Spirit came to them, their witness was not to be confined to Jerusalem but was to go to the ends of the earth.

Acts 2 records the coming of this Holy Spirit power at Pentecost. The most important fact of Pentecost is not the sound of the violent wind or the tongues of fire, or even the Christians speaking in other tongues, but that the people heard the wonders of God. Because this was declared in the power of the Holy Spirit, three thousand were brought to a saving knowledge of the Lord Jesus. This continued to be the main feature of Acts. Miracles took place which astounded the people, but it was preaching in the power of the Spirit that caused them to cry out, 'What must we do?' The answer was always, 'Repent!'

The emerging Church experienced a great sense of oneness (2:42–47; 4:32–37). There was love, fellowship and growth but there were also problems. Some of these were external, such as the opposition of the Sadducees in chapter 4, but the more serious problems were internal, as we see recorded in chapters 5:1–10 and 6:1–7.

Ananias and Sapphira were members of the Church. That meant that they had professed faith in Christ, had been baptized, and the Church recognized them as true believers. Yet those two conspired together to lie to the Church, which was in effect nothing less than lying to the Holy Spirit (5:3). 'The plan was concocted by Ananias, with Sapphira his wife. There is concert in evil. It is not the sudden impulse of an unguarded moment. It argues an extreme hardness of heart when two persons, united by the tenderest bond, plan a lie together, and engage to support each other in carrying it out' (William Arnot).

This incident could have devastated the young Church and it certainly served as an example of the seriousness of sin (5:11). 'Unless the church find or generate truth, it will not overcome the world; it will sink as in a mire. At the outset a pen of iron and the point of a diamond must be employed to print truth, as on the rock forever. A blow must be dealt against falsehood, which will vibrate down to the end of time, leaving all men to know that the lie which is cherished in the bosom of the world must be cast out from the body of Christ' (William Arnot).

Whether Ananias and Sapphira were ever truly converted will always be open to doubt, but the problem that arose in Acts 6 was among men and women of whom there is no doubt that they were true believers. This was potentially more dangerous than the Ananias and Sapphira incident because it could have split the Church on nationalistic issues. But with great wisdom the apostles dealt quickly and fairly with this powder-keg, and the result was that the Word of God spread (6:7).

'The falsehood of Ananias, and the discontent of the Hellenists, grew in different compartments of the same field. One root of bitterness grew in the givers, and another in the receivers. Both are recorded, that Christians in subsequent ages might be warned on either side' (William Arnot).

The persecution continued and, in chapter 7, Stephen became the first Christian martyr. To lose a man of his outstanding qualities in such a way could have devastated the Church. But God is good, and from the depths of chapter 7 we are taken to the soaring heights of remarkable blessing in chapter 8. Then the most amazing thing of all happens in chapter 9 and Saul of Tarsus, the great enemy of the gospel, is converted. This was so unexpected that at first the Christians in Jerusalem did not believe that he was now one of them (9:26). The strength of Paul's opposition to Christianity is hinted at in v.31. With that opposition now ceased, the Church enjoyed a time of peace. Meanwhile, Peter continued his ministry. Chapters 10 and 11 were of vital importance for the fulfilling of Christ's command in 1:8, that the gospel was to be preached to the ends of the earth. Up to this point there had been very little effort made to preach to gentiles, so God once more takes the initiative. Firstly, He gives Peter the vision (10:9–16) of the sheet from heaven. The purpose of this was to overcome Peter's Jewish prejudice against preaching to the Roman centurion, Cornelius. Peter preaches to the centurion and Cornelius is saved. A new understanding begins to dawn upon Peter (10:34–36) but the other apostles still have their Jewish anti-gentile prejudice and

Peter has to convince them otherwise (11:1–17). They are convinced and the true breadth of God's grace is for the first time recognized – 'God has even granted the Gentiles repentance unto life' (11:18).

This was a great breakthrough but in spite of 11:18, we read in the next verse that they were still preaching only to Jews. The real breakthrough comes at Antioch when the gospel is preached to the Greeks and a great number of these gentiles believe. Antioch then becomes the missionary Church from which the first two missionaries are sent out (13:1–3). 'The preparations for the Gentile mission were at last complete. There was a missionary church and there was a great missionary. At last the work could begin. It began, however, not by human initiative, but by direct command of God' (J. Gresham Machen).

Paul's first missionary journey is recorded in chapters 13 and 14. On the journey there was opposition (13:8) and disappointment (13:13, see also 15:37, 38) but there was also great blessing, and it was a thrilling report that Paul and Barnabas had to give to the Church at Antioch on their return (13:27).

This first venture with the gospel into Asia Minor raised, for some, a very serious problem and this is dealt with at the Council of Jerusalem in chapter 15. The issue is stated very clearly in v.1. Would the gentiles have to become Jews if they were to become Christians? The Judaizers said 'yes'. Paul and Barnabas said 'no'. The dispute was settled at Jerusalem, where Paul and the Judaizers argued their respective cases before the apostles. 'After speeches by Peter and by James, the leaders of the Jerusalem church promulgated a formal decree in which the Judaizers were repudiated, the work of Paul and Barnabas approved, and the freedom of the gentiles from the law clearly recognized. According to the decree, it is true, the Gentile Christians were to observe four rules, of which three were apparently ceremonial rather than moral in character. But these prohibitions were not imposed upon the Gentile Christians as though a part of the Jewish law were necessary to salvation. The prohibitions were rather intended simply to help solve the practical problem of mixed communities where Jews and gentiles were united in the same church. It was not intended – even Paul did not demand it – that Jewish Christians should give up the keeping of the law. But how could they keep the law in churches where there were Gentiles? The very association with the Gentiles would be a violation of the law. The four prohibitions of the apostolic decree were intended to remove at least a part of the difficulty. Out of love for their Jewish Christian brethren, and also in order to win non-Christian Jews to the faith, the Gentile Christians in these mixed communities were to refrain from those elements of Gentile custom which would be most abhorrent to the Jewish mind' (J. Gresham Machen).

Chapters 15:36–21:16 describe the second and third missionary journeys as the gospel is taken further afield still, and eventually into Europe for the first time. This covers a period of about ten years. When the apostle returns to Jerusalem, he is warmly received by the Christians there, but he is soon in trouble with the Jews (21:27–36). He is arrested and such is the hatred of the Jews that he has to be moved from Jerusalem to Caesarea for his own safety. Two years were spent in prison at Caesarea (chapters 24 and 26) until Paul is dispatched to Rome to plead his case before Caesar.

The two years' imprisonment were not wasted by Paul. He took every opportunity to preach the gospel and held nothing back as he preached righteousness, self-control and judgement to the notoriously wicked Felix. The man trembled before the power of the Word of God, but he remained unsaved (24:25–26). His successor, Festus, dismissed the gospel as insanity (26:24) but King Agrippa was not left untouched. His words in 26:28 have been variously translated and interpreted to mean a trivial jest, bitter sarcasm, a burst of anger or sincere conviction. From the context, in which Paul is convinced that Agrippa believes the Scriptures (v.27), it would seem that the Authorized Version, 'Almost thou persuadest me to be a Christian', depicting sincere conviction, is the best interpretation.

The journey to Rome (chapters 27 and 28) is dramatic and perilous. The storm, the shipwreck and the incident with the snake on Malta all demonstrate what a remarkable man Paul was, and that God's hand was undoubtedly upon him. He had only been in Rome for three days when he started to try and win the Roman Jews to Christ. The book ends abruptly with Paul boldly preaching and teaching about the Lord Jesus Christ.

'This last testimony uttered by the apostle throws light on the structure and design of the Book of the Acts. The history is designed to exhibit the transition of the kingdom from Israel as a nation to the whole human family. When this transference has been completed the historian's work is done. Here, accordingly, the record abruptly closes. The final note, as in other melodies, is the key-note: Christ rejected by Israel, to whom he came, is offered to the Gentiles. Henceforth all distinctions are levelled except one: the distinction between those who believe, and those who believe not, in the only begotten Son of God' (William Arnot).

STUDY MATERIAL

Studies in Acts by William Arnot (Kregel, 1978).
The Message of Acts in *The Bible Speaks Today* series, by John Stott (Inter-Varsity Press, 1990).

෨ 9 ෨

Things Hard to Understand

The Apostle Peter describes Paul's letters as containing 'some things that are hard to understand' (2 Pet. 3:16). Many young Christians would agree with that and tend therefore to avoid Paul's letters as too difficult. But in the same passage Peter said that Paul wrote 'with the wisdom that God gave him'. So to neglect Paul's writings is to deprive ourselves of this God-given wisdom. John Calvin reminds us that 'we are not forbidden to read Paul's epistles because they contain some things hard and difficult to be understood, but that, on the contrary, they are commended to us, provided we bring a calm and teachable mind'.

It is understandable that people new to the Christian faith find Paul's writings rather awesome. But Paul wrote 13 of the 27 New Testament books, so we cannot avoid them. Do not make the mistake of thinking that as a young Christian you can afford to leave these books for a few years and in the meantime read something easier. You need to learn early on in your Christian life to love these epistles for what they are – part of the inspired word of God.

This section of the book should help new Christians to understand Paul and his letters. It is meant to be a simple introduction to the Pauline Epistles, and its purpose is that those new to the faith may come to love the truths so marvellously expressed in these 13 letters, and in so doing be able to say with Paul, 'Oh, the depth of the riches of the wisdom and knowledge of God! How unsearchable his judgments, and his paths beyond tracing out! Who has known the mind of the Lord? Or who has been his counsellor? Who has ever given to God, that God should repay him? For from him and through him and to him are all things. To him be the glory for ever! Amen' (Rom. 11:33–36).

೦೦ 10 ೦೦

Paul, the Man and His Letters

A second-century writer described Paul as 'a man little of stature, partly bald, with crooked legs, of vigorous physique, with eyes set close together and nose somewhat hooked'. How accurate this description is no-one knows, but Paul himself quotes others as saying that 'in person he is unimpressive and his speaking amounts to nothing' (2 Cor. 10:10). Whatever he was physically, this man was a spiritual giant.

Paul was born in the city of Tarsus, which he describes as 'no ordinary city' (Acts 21:39). By this he may have meant that it was one of the great university cities of the Roman Empire, or perhaps like most citizens of Tarsus, he was proud of the fact that the Roman general, Mark Anthony, granted it the status of a 'free city' in 42 BC. Paul was a Jew, but he was born a citizen of Rome (Acts 22:28), which indicates that his father was probably a Roman citizen.

Though Tarsus was famous for its schools, his father sent him to be educated at Jerusalem under a noted rabbi, Gamaliel. It is almost certain that Paul was in Jerusalem during the time of the death of Jesus. He may have seen Jesus at this time, though he never mentions it. What is certain is that he hated everything that Jesus Christ stood for – read Galatians 1:13, Philippians 3:6 and Acts 26:9–11.

Yet, amazingly, this man became a Christian. It was no gradual conversion but a thunderbolt from God that floored him on the road to Damascus (Acts 9). He met the Lord Jesus Christ, and in so doing he was confronted with the true glory of God for the first time in his life. 'The crucified Teacher whom Paul had despised was really risen from the dead, the Lord of glory, the true Messiah of Israel. The shameful death on the cross was really the divine sacrifice for the sins of men. All of Paul's life crumbled away beneath him. In miserable blindness he groped his way into Damascus, a poor wretched, broken-spirited man! All his zeal had been nothing but rebellion against the King of Israel. Yet Jesus had appeared to him, not to put him to shame, but to save him. The poor, bewildered, broken-spirited rabbi became the most influential man in the history of the world!' (Gresham Machen).

Paul was a new man in every way. When he became a Christian, he lost much. Friends, prospects, popularity all went, but he considered them nothing but rubbish (Phil. 3:8) compared to what he gained.

Within days of conversion, Paul was preaching Christ (Acts 9:20). And the rest of his life was spent in this great activity. From the Church in Antioch, Paul was set apart for missionary work (Acts 13:1–3). On three missionary journeys he established churches in many cities. Most of the epistles were written to these churches.

'The aim of Paul's letters was essentially practical. They were not composed as literature, nor designed to set up a system, but were written to encourage and help and to guide those to whom they were addressed' (*The New Bible Handbook*).

The impact of these letters on young churches was immense. Even his enemies had to admit that 'his letters are weighty and forceful' (2 Cor. 10:10). By the nature of events, the early churches were made up of new and immature Christians; consequently they were a prey for false teachers with heretical doctrines, and also they were churches with many internal problems. Most of the letters were written, therefore, to deal with a particular problem existing at the time. But the principles laid down by Paul, under the inspiration of the Holy Spirit, and the doctrines expounded are of lasting and inestimable worth to the Church of our day.

All Paul's letters were written during a period of less than twenty years from AD 50 to about AD 68. It is not possible to be absolutely accurate concerning the dates when the various books were written because the New Testament does not mention dates. But using information found in the Scriptures and other historical facts, some dates can be arrived at and may be taken to be accurate to within a couple of years at the most. What is certain is that most of the epistles were written before the earliest of the Gospels. The order of the books in the New Testament might lead us to assume that the four Gospels were all written before Paul began his letters. But this is not so. Mark was written about AD 55–60, Matthew and Luke some time between AD 65 and 70, and John probably not until about AD 90. This means that a great deal of the first written account of the life and teaching of Jesus comes from Paul. For instance, Matthew, Mark and Luke all tell us of how Jesus instituted the Lord's Supper, but Paul's account in 1 Corinthians 11 was written before these.

Galatians, 1 Thessalonians and 2 Thessalonians were the first epistles to be written (about AD 50), and probably at Corinth while Paul was on his second missionary journey.

1 Corinthians was written about AD 53–54, probably from Ephesus, and two years or so later the second Corinthian epistle was penned. The Roman letter also belongs to this period, about AD 57.

Colossians, Philemon, Ephesians and Philippians are known as the 'prison epistles', because it is generally believed that they were written when Paul was in prison in Rome between AD 61 and 63.

The last three of Paul's letters were written towards the end of his life (AD 63–67). 1 and 2 Timothy and Titus are known as the 'pastoral epistles'.

Outline of Paul's Life

As we have seen, the dates can only be approximate, but they help us to see where the letters fit into the apostle's life and ministry.

AD 34	Paul's conversion (Acts 9:1–9)
AD 37–46	Paul in Damascus; Arabia; Jerusalem; Tarsus; Antioch; Jerusalem again (Acts 9:19–30; Gal. 1:15–17; Acts 11:25–26; Gal. 2:1)
AD 47	First missionary journey: Antioch; Cyprus; Antioch in Pisidia; Iconium; Lystra; Derbe (Acts 13 & 14)
AD 48	Council of Jerusalem (Acts 15)
AD 48–51	Second missionary journey: Antioch; Cilicia; Derbe; Lystra; Macedonia; Philippi; Thessalonica; Berea; Athens; Corinth; Ephesus; Antioch (Acts 15:36; 18:22). **At Corinth he writes Galatians and 1 and 2 Thessalonians**

AD 53	Third missionary journey: Antioch; Galatia; Phrygia; Ephesus (stayed for three years, AD 54–57) (Acts 18:23–19:41) **Wrote 1 Corinthians at Ephesus**
AD 57–58	Third missionary journey continues **Wrote 2 Corinthians, probably at Philippi** Macedonia; Troas; Miletus; Rhodes; Tyre; Caesarea; Jerusalem (Acts 20:1–21:17) **Wrote Romans, probably at Corinth**
AD 58–60	Two years' imprisonment at Jerusalem and Caesarea (Acts 21:27–26:32)
AD 60–61	Journey to Rome (Acts 27)
AD 61–63	In prison in Rome (Acts 28) **Wrote Colossians, Philemon, Ephesians, Philippians**
AD 63–65	Acts finishes in AD 63 with Paul in prison at Rome, but it is highly likely that he was released from prison and had a few more years of missionary work. During those years, he wrote **1 Timothy and Titus**
AD 66–67	The second period of imprisonment in Rome. He wrote **2 Timothy** shortly before his death.

ᐁᔥ II ᐁᔥ

Romans

Rome was the capital of a vast empire that stretched from Britain to Arabia. How the church was founded there is not known. The Roman Catholic tradition that Peter was the founder has no evidence to support it from either Scripture or history. 'There were various ways in which the gospel could easily have been carried to Rome. Roman Jews must often have returned to the feasts at Jerusalem. Some of them were present on the day of Pentecost, Acts 2:10. Between the mother country and the large Jewish colony at Rome there must have been many opportunities of intercourse' (J. Gresham Machen).

If the church at Rome was founded by Jews, the evidence seems to indicate that by the time Paul wrote Romans, the church there consisted mainly of gentiles. At the time of writing, Paul had never visited Rome. 'The Epistle was written from Corinth during Paul's third journey, not long after he finished his prolonged sojourn in Ephesus; just before he took to Jerusalem the collection for the poor saints, and when he was hoping for the first time to visit Rome on his way to Spain, i.e. about AD 56 or 57 (Acts 19:21; 20:2–3; Romans 15:23–28). Since Paul commends Phoebe to his readers (16:1–2), it would appear that she was about to go to Rome. She has commonly been regarded from early times, as the bearer of the Epistle' (*The New Bible Handbook*).

We are not sure why Paul wrote this letter other than perhaps it was meant to pave the way for his visit, but it is certainly a supreme declaration of the gospel of salvation through the sovereign grace of God.

CONTENTS

'No book or section of Scripture has played a more important part in the history of the church and some of its most notable leaders than Paul's Epistle to the Romans. It was through reading some verses at the end of its thirteenth chapter that the great Saint Augustine was converted. His majestic figure towers over the story of the church from the fifth century onwards. It was through being enlightened as to the real meaning of the seventeenth verse of the first chapter, with its teaching on justification by faith only, that Martin Luther was delivered from his bondage and became the leader of the Protestant Reformation. The same doctrine, as expounded by Luther, led to the conversion of John Bunyan, the "Immortal Tinker of Bedford", and so gave us The Pilgrim's Progress and Grace Abounding. Similarly it was as he listened to a man reading from the Preface of Luther's Commentary on this epistle that John Wesley's heart was "strangely warmed" on the evening of 24th May 1738. The same has been the testimony of countless other less well-known Christians. Surely no further reasons are necessary for a most careful study of the contents of this epistle' (D. M. Lloyd-Jones).

SUMMARY

It is impossible to understand Romans without understanding Paul's use of the word 'righteousness'.

In 1:16 he states that the gospel is the power of God for salvation. Then in verse 17 he tells us why this is so. It is because 'in the gospel a righteousness from God is revealed' and made available to sinners. Because the wrath of God is revealed against man's unrighteousness, man's greatest need is for righteousness. Therefore the prime function of the gospel is not to make men happy but to make them righteous. You can be happy and go to hell, but you cannot be righteous and go to hell.

'The noun righteousness is especially characteristic of Romans where it is used 33 times, the next highest total being seven each in 2 Corinthians and Matthew. It is a term which must be understood carefully. With us it is an ethical virtue, as it was for the Greeks generally. But among the Hebrews righteousness was first and foremost a legal standing. The righteous were those who secured the verdict when they stood before God. This terminology applied even in an earthly court, and "the righteous" and "the wicked" in the Old Testament often mean much what we mean when we speak of "the innocent" and "the guilty" (Deut. 25:1). In the final analysis what matters is the verdict of the heavenly court, and the man who is ultimately righteous is the one who is acquitted when tried at the bar of God's justice' (Leon Morris).

Man in Sin

Man's problem is that 'there is no one righteous, not even one' (3:10). This is quite a staggering claim but Paul has proved its truth. In chapter 1, he considers the gentiles. They had nothing of the special advantages of the Jews. They had no God-given Scriptures, no God-sent prophets but they had enough of God's revelation in nature (1:19, 20) to render their sin inexcusable. That sin brought upon them the wrath of God (1:18) and note the terrible judgement of vv.24, 26 and 28 – 'God gave them over'. This means that God abandoned them to the consequences of their own sin.

In chapter 2, he considers the Jews. Though they had so many advantages and privileges (3:1, 2), they also were sinners under the wrath of God. Paul sums up the state of all men in 3:19 – the whole world is guilty before God. Then he repeats this in 3:23, 'There is no difference, for all have sinned'. Man has no righteousness and nothing that he can do (3:20) can gain him righteousness. The situation is hopeless. But in 3:21 Paul begins to expound the gospel that he first introduces in 1:16. Here is God's answer to man's problems. There is a righteousness from God, apart from anything that man can do, and it comes to us through faith in Jesus Christ (3:22).

Justification by Faith

Romans 3:21–26 is a thrilling description of God's complete answer to the ravages of sin:

Sin leaves us	*God's answer*
Guilty and condemned.....	Justification (v.24)
Enslaved and in bondage....	Redemption (v.24)
Spiritually impoverished with nothing to offer God.....	Grace (v.24)
Under divine wrath and judgement.....	Propitiation (AV) (v.25)
Deserving punishment.....	Christ's blood (v.25)

God's answer comes to us through faith in the Lord Jesus Christ and this provides us with the imputed or credited righteousness of Christ (4:3–8, 23–25).

We are pronounced righteous, but not on account of our own works. Christians do possess not their own righteousness but 'a righteousness of God'. This righteousness of God is received by faith. Faith is a gift from God whereby we are enabled to believe the gospel and receive this righteousness. 'But faith is not the act of God; it is not God who believes in Christ for salvation, it is the sinner. It is by God's grace that a person is able to believe, but faith is an activity on the part of the person and of him alone. In faith we receive and rest upon Christ alone for salvation' (John Murray).

Christ's righteousness becomes ours because of our union with Him. Before we were saved, we were 'without Christ' (Eph. 2:12), but now we are 'in Christ' (Eph. 1:1). This means that Christ is our Head, our Representative. In Adam we were guilty and condemned; in Christ we are justified and pardoned (Rom. 5:12–21).

A simple definition of justification is that it is the sovereign work of God whereby He declares the guilty sinner to be righteous on account of the rightful demands of the law being satisfied by Christ on his behalf. Let us examine this definition:

[56]

'sovereign work of God' – God does it all; the sinner plays no part at all (Rom. 3:24; 4:4, 5)

'declares' – the judge pronouncing a legal verdict

'guilty sinner' – guilty by nature (Eph. 2:1–3) and guilty by action (Rom. 3:10–23)

'righteous' – right with God (Rom. 5:1)

'demands of the law' – God's law demands eternal death for the sinner (Rom. 6:23)

'satisfied' – legally and justly satisfied by the atoning death of Jesus (Rom. 3:26; 5:18–21)

The benefits of justification are shown to us in chapter 5 and supreme among these is peace with God. There can be no peace with God unless the problems created by man's sin and guilt, and God's wrath on that sin, are dealt with. The Bible knows of no peace with God that bypasses the problem of man's sin and God's wrath. But this gospel of God's grace deals with all these things.

The aim of the gospel is to restore to man all that sin robbed him of. In Genesis 3 when Adam sinned, he lost essentially three things:

1. Peace with God – Genesis 3:8–10. He is afraid of God and hides from his Creator.
2. Access to God – Genesis 3:22–24. He is barred from the presence of God.
3. All hope for the future – Genesis 3:17–19. Temporal and spiritual blessings (Gen. 3:3) were withdrawn.

These three – peace, access and hope – are restored to us by justification (Rom. 5:1–2). In chapter 5, Paul teaches that all we lost in Adam is restored to us in Christ, plus the 'how much more' (vv. 15–17) of God's provision of grace and the gift of righteousness.

Living the Christian Life

The gospel does not stop at imputing or crediting Christ's righteousness to us (justification). God intends us to be changed people. He means us to live a new life free from the domination of sin (6:1–4). He wants us to be 'slaves to righteousness' (6:18).

[57]

'Our position, as Christians, is that we have been "enslaved to righteousness". This does not mean that we admire righteousness, nor that we desire to be righteous: it does not mean that we are attempting to be righteous, or attempting to practise righteousness daily in our daily life. It includes all these things but has a much wider content. What the Apostle says is, that we have become "slaves to righteousness" – nothing less. Not "servants", but "slaves" of righteousness! That means that we have come under the power and control and influence of righteousness. As once we were tyrannized over and ruled by, and governed by sin, we are now, we may say, tyrannized over and governed and ruled by righteousness itself. Furthermore, this is something that is true of every one of us from the moment of our regeneration. The Apostle is talking about Christians – any Christian. From the moment we are regenerate it is true to say of us that we are no longer slaves of sin; we are slaves of righteousness' (D. M. Lloyd-Jones).

Having received imputed righteousness and becoming a slave to righteousness does not mean that we are free from struggling with sin. Chapter 7 relates how real this struggle can be for a Christian. But in spite of the struggle and sometimes being overcome by sin, the glory of the gospel is that there is no condemnation for those in Christ (Rom. 8:1). This amazing eighth chapter starts with no condemnation and ends with no separation and sandwiched between them is the fact that because we are indwelt by the Holy Spirit, there are for us rich experiences of Christ.

'This is one of the great chapters in the Bible, and its teaching about the way the Holy Spirit operates in enabling the believer to defeat the forces of evil has always been recognized as of the utmost importance. There are problems in detail, but the main thrust is clear. Paul is saying that a new and wonderful life opens out before those who put their trust in Christ and that this depends heavily on the work of the Spirit of God' (Leon Morris).

'Chapters 9–11 of this epistle are interesting in a great many ways. They are interesting, for example, in their tremendous conception of the mystery of the divine will. The ninth chapter of Romans is a good corrective for any carelessness in our attitude toward God. After all, God is a mystery. How little we know of his eternal plan! We must ever tremble before him. Yet it is such a God who has invited us, through Christ, to hold communion with himself. There is the true wonder of the gospel – that it brings us

[58]

ROMANS

into fellowship, not with a God of our own devising, not with one who is a Father and nothing else, but with the awful, holy, mysterious Maker and Ruler of all things. The joy of the believer is the deepest of all joys. It is a joy that is akin to holy fear' (J. Gresham Machen).

The remaining chapters seek to apply the great gospel truths to everyday living. 'In view of God's mercy' (12:4) we should:

12:10	Be devoted to one another in brotherly love
13:7	Pay taxes if we owe them
13:13	Put on the armour of light
14:13	Stop passing judgement on one another
14:19	Make every effort to do what leads to peace
15:1	Bear with the failings of the weak

Paul sums everything up in 15:13 – 'May the God of hope fill you with all joy and peace as you trust in him, so that you may overflow with hope by the power of the Holy Spirit'.

STUDY MATERIAL

There are numerous excellent commentaries and expositions of Romans. Ultimately you may be wise to obtain the books written by Martyn Lloyd-Jones, John Murray and Leon Morris, but at the moment as young Christians buy and study just three books:

Romans by Geoffrey Wilson (Banner of Truth, 1977). Keep this as a reference book when you come across a verse that you do not understand.

The Gospel As It Really Is, by Stuart Olyott (Evangelical Press, 1979). Use Stuart Olyott's book to read through Romans. There are sections of the epistle set to be read and then about six pages of explanation on each section. This is ideal for daily readings and will take you through the epistle in twenty-six days.

The New Testament. An Introduction to its Literature and History, by J. Gresham Machen (Banner of Truth, 1976). This superb book will help you immensely.

∾ 12 ∾

The Corinthian Epistles

Corinth of the first century was a Greek city famous for its culture, its prosperity and its immorality. 'The town was dominated by the temple of Aphrodite (goddess of love; what a contrast to 1 Corinthians 13!), built on the heights of the acropolis. Thousands of temple prostitutes, a large floating population, and the general racial hotch-potch, all contributed to Corinth's unsavoury name. The city was a by-word for excess and sexual licence. There was even a word for it: to Corinthianize' (*The Lion Handbook*). The church there was founded by Paul on his second missionary journey (Acts 18), when he stayed in the city for 18 months. It was no easy task preaching the gospel in such an evil city, and perhaps even Paul had begun to waver when God encouraged him in a special way (Acts 18:9–11).

'I have many people in this city' does not mean that there were already many Christians there. Rather, God was encouraging Paul, telling him that there were many there who would become Christians as a result of his preaching.

'The Lord knows those that are his, yea, and those that shall be his; for it is by his work upon them that they become his, and known unto him are all his works. I have them, though they yet know me not, though yet they are led captive by Satan at his will; for the Father has given them to me, to be a seed to serve me; I have them written in the book of life; I have their names down, and of all that were given me I will lose none; I have them, for I am sure to have them: "whom he did predestinate, those he called." In this city, though it be a profane wicked city, full of impurity, and the more so for a temple of Venus there, to which there was a great resort, yet in this heap, that seems to be all chaff, there is wheat; in this ore, that seems to be all dross, there is gold. Let us not despair

[60]

concerning any place, when even in Corinth Christ had much people' (Matthew Henry).

1 Corinthians

The church at Corinth was remarkable in many ways. It abounded in spiritual life and vitality, yet it was full of problems. By the time Paul wrote the first epistle (AD 53–54) the church had been in existence for only two or three years. It was young and immature – 'mere infants in Christ' (3:1).

The letter was written because Paul had heard some disturbing reports about the Corinthian Church (1:11), and also to answer certain questions sent from Corinth by letter to the apostle (7:1). For these reasons the letter is of great importance because it shows us the internal problems of a New Testament church more than any other in Scripture. 'It was all very well for the humble tradesmen or the down-trodden slaves of Corinth to listen to the glorious message of the one holy and merciful God and the new, free brotherhood of his children. But after the first flush of joy, the stern facts of life came pressing in again with double force. It was all very well to turn from idols to serve the living and true God. But the whole life of that day was suffused with idolatry. How could the Christian avoid contamination? Where should he draw the line? The enthusiasm of the early church could not deliver men from the petty problems of human life; and in many respects these problems were even far more perplexing then than they are today. How ought Christian faith to work out in practise? – that was a difficult question for the Corinthian Christians to answer. Only by understanding these practical difficulties can we sympathize with the Church's failures – and only so can we appreciate, too, the full wonder of her final triumph' (Gresham Machen).

CONTENTS

[61]

SUMMARY

The first six chapters contain the response of Paul to certain disturbing reports that he had received about the church at Corinth (1:11). The reports revealed two very serious problems in this church. Firstly, it was not united but divided into various factions (chapters 1–4); and secondly, there was gross sexual immorality, and a total lack of church discipline to deal with it (chapters 5 & 6).

The party spirit centred around three prominent leaders and the Lord Jesus Christ (1:12). Paul was the founder of the Corinthian church; Apollos was a very powerful and eloquent preacher; Peter's following probably came from the Jewish Christians. For reasons that do not appear to be doctrinal but more of intellectual pride, many Christians lined up behind these great men. The men themselves were not involved. They were not touting for support. Then there were those who disapproved of following mere men. These neutrals declared that they followed Christ alone. 'These neutrals were probably the worst class in the congregation, as is commonly the case with those who claim to be Christians to the exclusion of all others' (Charles Hodge). Paul represents this spirit as the result of worldly thinking and spiritual immaturity (3:1–9). He urges them to stop boasting about men (3:21–22), and not to 'take pride in one man over against another' (4:6).

While all this strife about men was going on, sexual immorality was allowed to go undisciplined. The seriousness of the sin is expressed in 5:1, 'of a kind that does not occur even among pagans'. 'The offence was that a man had married his step-mother. His father's wife is a Scriptural periphrase [roundabout way of speaking] for step-mother, Lev. 18:8. That it was a case of marriage is to be inferred from the uniform use of the phrase *to have a woman* in the New Testament, which means, to marry.

[62]

Matt. 14:4; 22:28, 1 Cor. 7:2, 29' (Charles Hodge). As this sin had
been allowed to go on, the whole church was endangered (5:6).
The only remedy was to put the guilty man out of the fellowship of
the church. Notice the strength of Paul's language:

5:5   hand this man over to Satan
5:11   you must not associate with anyone who calls himself a
        brother but is sexually immoral; with such a man do not
        even eat.
5:13   expel the wicked man from your number

Discipline is essential for the purity of the church but Paul is
also very concerned for the restoration of the sinner: 'and his spirit
saved on the day of the Lord' (5:5). 'The nature and end of
judgement or sentence must be corrective, not vindictive; for
healing, not destruction' (John Owen).

The divisions and immorality were not the only problems in the
Corinthian church. In chapter 6, Paul rebukes them severely for
not being able to settle disputes between themselves. Christians
suing Christians in the law courts before ungodly judges is an
abomination.

The testimony and reputation of this church before the citizens
of Corinth could not have been very high. Yet these problems were
not mentioned in the letter that they wrote to Paul asking for
advice. Was it because they were too embarrassed to raise such
matters, or was it that they were not too bothered about these
things?

In chapter 7, the apostle begins to deal with the matters
mentioned in their letter. Is there a link between the problems that
they write about and the ones not mentioned? For instance, the
problem of the divisions in the church. From 11:17 to 14:40 Paul
deals with some causes of strife which are not really doctrinal but
based on pride and lack of love and concern for each other (see
11:20–22; 12:21–26; 13:4–7; 14:20). The immorality problem in
chapter 5 stemmed from a man marrying his step-mother (his
father's wife), which Scripture clearly forbids (Lev. 18:6–8). If the
Christian attitude to marriage outlined in chapter 7 was acted
upon, it would rectify this problem.

The law-suits issue arose because Christians insisted on their
rights and were not prepared to accept wrongs (6:7–8). Note how

this attitude stands compared to the teaching on the exercise of freedom in chapters 8 and 9. If the Corinthians had really believed 10:23–24, it would have been impossible to sue each other in the courts. Paul's words there read: 'Everything is permissible – but not everything is beneficial. Everything is permissible – but not everything is constructive. Nobody should seek his own good, but the good of others.'

It is significant that in dealing with the contentious issue of spiritual gifts in chapters 12 and 14, Paul finds it necessary to place between these chapters the great statement on love in chapter 13. This is always the true Christian answer to strife. Note 13:5 – love 'is not easily angered, it keeps no record of wrongs'.

A problem at Corinth which does seem to have been primarily doctrinal is that of the resurrection of the dead. There were some in the church who said that there was no resurrection (15:12). In the 15th chapter, one of the great chapters of Scripture, Paul answers this error. It deals not only with the fact of the literal, physical, bodily resurrection of Jesus, but also of the bodily resurrection of all Christians. 'The whole system of Christianity rests upon the fact that "Christ is risen from the dead . . . if Christ be not risen, then shall we not rise; but if he be risen then they who are asleep in Christ have not perished, but in their flesh shall surely behold their God." Thus, the silver thread of resurrection runs through all the believer's blessings, from his regeneration onwards to his eternal glory, and binds them together. How important then will this glorious fact be in his estimation, and how will he rejoice that beyond a doubt it is established, that "now is Christ risen from the dead"' (C. H. Spurgeon).

2 Corinthians

This was written about AD 57 from a town in Macedonia, probably Philippi.

The relationship between the two epistles is not altogether clear but the following is a possible explanation of what happened.

After writing 1 Corinthians, things in the church there became worse rather than better. Paul heard about this while he was still at Ephesus. He then went to Corinth for a short second visit. This is not mentioned in Acts but is strongly alluded to in 2 Corinthians 2:1. This 'painful visit' could not refer to his first visit when he spent 18 months in the city and founded the church. The pain was caused by the Corinthians refusing to listen to Paul's advice on a matter of church discipline. On returning to Ephesus, Paul wrote a sharp letter to Corinth (2:4). This letter, of which we have no copy, is referred to again in chapter 7 and verse 8.

From these verses in chapters 2 and 7, it is obvious that writing as he did was not easy for Paul. He loved the Corinthian Christians deeply and it grieved him to have to rebuke them severely. So he is anxious to know how they respond to the letter. 'It must have been an anxious time for Paul. He had spent years in founding the Corinthian church. Apparently it had been the most successful work of his life. He had put his very soul into it. Yet it seemed to be all in vain. The church was in open rebellion. Immorality was freely tolerated. False apostles were being allowed to lead. To all this maddening anxiety was added a terrible personal danger. In Asia, a short time before the epistle was written, Paul had despaired of his life. Having escaped by the mercy of God, he had gone to Troas, eager for news from Corinth. But Titus had not returned. Paul could stand it no longer. He went on into Macedonia. And there, at last, Titus met him – and brought good news! The Corinthians had been made repentant by Paul's letter. They were ready to punish the offender. The old devotion was restored' (J. Gresham Machen).

The good news that Titus brought (7:5–7) was a source of great joy to Paul, but the problems were not all over. In 2 Corinthians, Paul has to defend his calling and ministry against the accusations of some at Corinth.

CONTENTS

| 12:14–21 | An expression of Paul's love and concern for this church |
| 13:1–14 | Final warnings |

SUMMARY

This is a very personal and very passionate letter. Recent events had caused Paul deep anxiety, and he wanted the Corinthians to be fully aware of these things. There had been a very real danger of his losing his life (1:8, 9). This, coupled with his worry about how they had reacted to his letter (2:1–4), put strains on Paul that began to show. '2 Corinthians is perhaps the most intensely personal of all Paul's letters. We feel for ourselves the weight of his burden of care for all the churches (11:28): the depth of his love for them and his anguished concern for their spiritual progress. We see in personal terms the cost of his missionary programme: hardship, suffering, deprivation, humiliation, almost beyond human endurance. And we see unshakable faith shining through it all, transforming every circumstance' (*The Lion Handbook*).

Twice in chapter 4 (vv.1, 16), Paul says 'we do not lose heart'. Obviously, there were many reasons in the Corinthian church why he could have lost heart. Even though he had founded the church only a few years prior to this letter, there was in Corinth a very strong opposition to Paul.

This opposition said:

| 10:1 | Paul was bold when away but timid when with them |
| 10:10 | His letters contain strong words, but in person he is unimpressive and a very poor speaker (preacher) |

In chapter 11 the attack intensifies. They say that Paul is foolish (v.1), inferior (v.5), not a good speaker (v.6) and does not love them (v.11). They even suggest that he tricked and exploited them (12:16, 17). Behind these attacks were men that Paul sarcastically calls super-apostles (11:5; 12:11), and he exposes them for what they really are – false apostles (11:13–15). They boasted of great things but in reality had achieved nothing (10:12–18). Such men exploited everything to attack Paul's reputation with the Corinthians. This included his severe letter and even his failure to visit them.

[66]

Paul's answer to all this was to plead the reality of his love for them (11:11). This he had proved by the sacrifices that he had made on their behalf (11:7–10). Several times he mentions that he never took money from them. Apparently the false apostles were not so scrupulous and peddled the word of God for profit (2:17). He boasts of how he behaved among them (11:16–33). His track-record speaks for itself. And chapter 12, verses 1–10, is a remarkable answer to the experiences of the 'super-apostles'.

'Probably Paul would not even have bothered to answer these and other charges had not the gospel itself been at stake. The interlopers who were leading the Corinthian church astray were not only personally ambitious, they were preaching what Paul discerned to be a false gospel, another Jesus (2 Cor. 11:4). That left Paul no alternative but to enter the fray; and the way he does this, with wisdom, wit, humour, irony, winsomeness, yet also anguish, hurt and stunning emotional intensity, constitutes a marvellous case study in Christian leadership and the maintenance of Christian values and priorities' (Donald A. Carson).

With all this weighing heavily upon his mind, it is nothing short of remarkable that Paul in chapters 8 and 9, takes time to urge the Corinthians to collect money for the poor believers in Jerusalem. He regards the giving of money, not as a necessary evil, but as an act of grace (8:6, 7). And to encourage generosity, he uses the example of God's giving to us (8:9; 9:15). Very often these are used as great texts for gospel preaching, but their context is to urge Christians to give money to others in need.

STUDY MATERIAL

1 & 2 Corinthians by Geoffrey Wilson (Banner of Truth 1978, 1979).
Be Wise, 1 Corinthians by Warren Wiersbe (Scripture Press, 1983).
From Triumphalism to Maturity: a study of 2 Corinthians 10–13 by Donald Carson (Inter-Varsity Press, 1986).

ᦉ 13 ᦉ

Galatians

Galatia was a very large Roman province in what we now know as central Turkey. The epistle is therefore addressed to the *churches* in Galatia (1:2). These churches would include the ones at Pisidian Antioch, Iconium, Lystra and Derbe, which Paul had founded on his first missionary journey (Acts 13 & 14) in AD 47. They consisted mainly of gentiles, but these new Christians, converted through the true biblical gospel of justification by faith (2:15–16), had been infiltrated by 'Judaizers', that is, Jews who professed faith in Christ. These men taught what Paul calls 'a different gospel – which is really no gospel at all' (1:6–7). They said that justification by faith was not enough to make us Christians. Their teaching is spelled out in Acts 15:1 – 'Unless you are circumcised, according to the custom taught by Moses, you cannot be saved'. 'There were three main points at issue between Paul and the Judaizers, and they are still vital issues in the church today. The first is the question of authority: how do we know what and whom to believe or disbelieve? The second is the question of salvation: how can we get right with God, receiving the forgiveness of our sins and being restored to His favour and fellowship? The third is the question of holiness: how can we control the sinful desires of our fallen nature and live a life of righteousness and love? Addressing himself to these questions, Paul devotes approximately the first two chapters of the Epistle to the question of authority, chapters 3 and 4 to the question of salvation, and chapters 5 and 6 to the question of holiness' (John R. W. Stott).

Some of the Galatians believed the false teachers. It is because of this that Paul, about AD 50 whilst at Corinth, writes what is probably his first letter contained in the New Testament. He writes fiercely and with great passion (1:6; 3:1). He does so because the truth of the gospel is at stake, and also because he loves these Galatians and cares deeply for them (4:19–20). They were among his first converts and he cannot bear to see them deluded.

So the sovereign grace of God and justification by faith alone must be put to them again. Thus, the theme of Galatians is a strong denunciation of false doctrine and a positive assertion of justification by faith alone. 'In the Galatian Epistle Paul personally combats this subversive teaching, and not long afterwards the Council of Jerusalem officially outlawed it, but to win the victory over legalism was to cost the apostle a life-long struggle against these "zealots for the law" whose ubiquitous activities threatened to stifle the faith of the infant church.

'Of the Epistle's importance there is happily no doubt whatever, for as Luther so rightly insisted, the mastery of its message is basic to a true understanding of the Christian faith. In this brief letter there is distilled for us the quintessence of Paul's gospel. Here we are brought face to face with a man whose burning words express the measure of his care for the purity of that gospel and for the safety of his readers' (Geoffrey B. Wilson).

CONTENTS

SUMMARY

There is a sense of urgency right throughout Galatians and it starts in the first verses. There are no pleasant words of greeting, as in most of the epistles; instead, Paul goes straight to the heart of the problem (1:6). Note the strength of Paul's words in 1:6–9. He very deliberately repeats the words 'let him be eternally condemned'.

The strength of the apostle's feeling is not because someone dares to disagree with him, but because the gospel that he preached was not his own invention but something that he had received by revelation from Christ (1:11–12). Therefore, the glory of the Lord Jesus was at stake, as well as the eternal salvation of men and women. Paul was fired up, and had every reason for being so.

He begins to defend his gospel by first of all defending his apostolic authority (1:11–2:21). He was not dependent for his authority upon the other apostles. Indeed, 'so independent was his authority that on one occasion he could even rebuke the chief of the original apostles himself' (Gresham Machen).

In chapter 3, Paul gets down to the heart of the matter, and he uses a word used nowhere else in the New Testament – 'bewitched'. So clearly was the gospel demonstrated to them and so clear was the operation of the Holy Spirit in saving them, that it seemed as if there was some outside supernatural force working to beguile them, to bewitch them.

The Galatians' problem was: were they saved by observing the law or by grace through faith? Paul takes them back to Abraham to show that even this great man was saved by faith (3:6–14). Paul has answered the Judaizers from the Old Testament and shown their teaching to be wrong. His argument is that it is impossible to keep the law totally, but that is what the law demands. He quotes Deuteronomy 27:26 (3:10); note here the word 'everything'. Failure to do everything that the law demands brings us under the curse of the law. That is, under its rightful punishment. So, far from saving us, the law actually condemns us. The only one who can save us is Christ. He alone can redeem sinners from the curse of the law (3:13).

Other examples are drawn from everyday life and from the Old Testament to make the same point. Paul sets before the Galatians two things: the promise of God and the law of God. These are not opposed to each other (3:21) but their purposes are different. First of all, God in his grace gave Abraham a promise (Gen. 12:1–3). It was an act of divine grace which Abraham did nothing to merit. But the promise did not only involve Abraham but also his seed. That seed is Christ (3:16) and those in Christ. This is the basis of God's covenant with mankind. Four hundred and thirty years later, God gave us His law, but this does not change His covenant (3:15). What, then, was the purpose of the law?

It was added. Added to what? To the covenant of promise. To that which had always been God's only way of accepting sinners. Why was it added? Paul has already established in v.15 that nothing can be added to change the terms or essence of the covenant. The law was added by God because of human sin. Man in his sin so despised the promises of God that he tossed them aside as if they were cheap, tawdry things. Something was needed to show man what he was; to awaken him to a sense of his own sin and guilt. Something was needed to show man how precious are the grace and promises of God. That something was the law.

The law gave man an objective and infallible standard by which he could measure himself. In Romans 5:20 Paul says that the law was added so that sin might increase. He means that the law acts like a magnifying glass. It increases or enlarges and exposes sin. It does not produce anything; it merely shows up very clearly what is there. It can reveal sin but it cannot deal with it. Only Christ can deal with sin. Therefore to rely on the law as the means of salvation is totally to misunderstand the purpose of the law, which is to lead us to Christ (3:24) by convicting us of our sin and turning us to the Lord Jesus Christ as the only Saviour.

Finally, Paul concludes the central section of the Epistle by emphasizing the gravity of the crisis, Gal. 5:1–12. Do not be deceived. Circumcision, as the Judaizers advocate it, is no innocent thing; it means the acceptance of a law-religion. You must choose either the law or grace; you cannot have both! (J. Gresham Machen).

Salvation by faith, not law, does not mean that the law of God has no place in the Christian's life. 'Christian liberty is not liberty to do what we like, but what Christ likes' (William Still). The entire law is summed up in one sentence: 'love your neighbour as yourself' (5:14). This only becomes possible if we live under the power and influence of the Holy Spirit, and then the beautiful fruit of the Spirit (5:22, 23) is manifest in our lives.

The fruit of the Spirit is nothing to do with a person's natural temperament. It is true that a man may be naturally patient and kind, but what Paul is dealing with here is the fruit which is the sole product of the Holy Spirit working in a person. It is the result of regeneration, when by the work of the Holy Spirit we become spiritually alive and are no longer the slaves of sin. Paul contrasts the fruit of the Spirit with 'the acts of the sinful nature' (5:19).

[71]

Regeneration frees us from the compulsive power of the sinful nature. In Christ we have a freedom to say 'no' to sin and to keep in step with the Spirit. This means to live according to the new nature that salvation has earned us. The Christian is a new creation in Christ, therefore he should live in the reality of that.

'The abiding value of the Epistle is its exposition of the nature of Christianity. It shows the gulf between legalism and the religion of the Spirit. Legalistic religion, since it dispenses with regeneration, is attractive and intelligible to the natural man. But it is a subtle and persistent enemy of true Christian faith. Over against it, Paul affirms that regeneration is the fundamental of Christianity (6:15), and that love is the practical expression of this change of heart' (*The New Bible Handbook*).

STUDY MATERIAL

Galatians by Geoffrey Wilson (Banner of Truth, 1979).
The Message of Galatians by John Stott in *The Bible Speaks Today* series (Inter-Varsity Press, 1960).

෨ 14 ෨

Ephesians

'As we approach this Epistle I confess freely that I do so with considerable temerity. It is very difficult to speak of it in a controlled manner because of its greatness and because of its sublimity. Many have tried to describe it. One writer has described it as "the crown and climax of Pauline theology". Another has said that it is "the distilled essence of the Christian religion, the most authoritative and most consummate compendium of our holy Christian faith". What language! And it is by no means exaggerated' (D. M. Lloyd-Jones).

Paul spent three years at Ephesus (AD 54–57) and he obviously had a great love for this church which he founded. It is not surprising, therefore, that during his imprisonment at Rome (AD 61–63), his thoughts turn to those saints and he writes to them this most beautiful letter.

The church at Ephesus was like any other church in that it had its problems, but at the time that this epistle was written, there appeared to be no major difficulty and the letter is more general than, for instance, Galatians. Some think it was a circular letter sent to Ephesus and other churches in the area. As Ephesus was the capital of the Roman province of Asia, this is quite possible. The fact that it was not written to deal with any particular problem perhaps gives Ephesians a special value. 'In many respects Ephesians reads more like a sermon – in some parts more like a prayer or a doxology – than a letter written to meet some special need in a Church or group of Churches. It is like a sermon on the greatest and widest theme possible for a Christian sermon – the eternal purpose of God, which He is fulfilling through His Son Jesus Christ, and working out in and through the Church' (Francis Foulkes).

STEPPING-STONES

CONTENTS

SUMMARY

The epistle to the Ephesians presents us with a worthy and exalted view of God. Paul starts by describing himself as being an apostle 'by the will of God'. But he does not stop there. If we are Christians, it is only because God chose us (1:4), predestined and adopted us (1:5). Our redemption is 'according to his good pleasure' (1:9). God works to a set purpose (1:9), to a plan which embraces everything (1:11), and our salvation is ultimately 'for the praise of his glory' (1:12).

'The lofty terms in which Paul extols the grace of God towards the Ephesians are intended to rouse their hearts to gratitude, to set them all on flame, to fill them even to overflowing with this disposition' (John Calvin).

The language of chapter 1 is rich and lavish but in no way inappropriate or exaggerated. It must surely cause us to gasp in astonishment at the wonder of God's great love, grace and power. Paul himself is excited as he contemplates what God has done for us. There is nothing ordinary or matter-of-fact about this and the same approach continues in chapter 2. 'The deep feeling continues, as is evident from such expressions as rich mercy . . . great love . . . surpassing riches of grace. This, too, as well as in chapter 1, is the language of gratitude and adoration' (William Hendriksen).

Chapter 2 is one of the greatest statements of the gospel in the New Testament. 'It deals with the profoundest and most elevating themes of the Bible. It shows us man's desperate need, it unfolds the glory of God's grace, the wonder of the cross of Christ, the breaking down of middle walls of partition, and the reconciliation of Jews and Gentiles, and all others who believe in the Lord Jesus Christ, in the kingdom of God' (D. M. Lloyd-Jones).

The contrast between the first three verses and the last four is quite amazing. The opening verses describe what the Ephesians were before they became Christians. Deadness, hopelessness and helplessness is the condition of all in sin. How different are verses 19–22! 'You are no longer' like that, says Paul. The transformation is almost unbelievable. What has caused it? The bridge between these two extreme conditions is vv.4–18, the grace of God.

The Christian is God's workmanship (v.10); faith is the result of God's mercy, grace and love working in our lives. There is no other possible explanation for the transformation that takes place at conversion. The gospel brings men into a state of peace with God and breaks down ancient barriers that separate man from man (vv.14–18). Peace is established between those who were enemies because both have been reconciled to God by the blood of the Lord Jesus Christ.

The wonder of all this moves Paul in chapter 3 to pray for the Ephesians. Notice the phrase 'for this reason' in v.1 and v.14. He starts to say something in v.1, then he stops and digresses for a while (vv.2–13) before he comes back to his original thought in v.14. This is not unusual in Paul's writings. He often goes off on a bypass before coming back to his main thought, but there is always a valid reason. The reason here is given us in v.13. Paul is writing this letter as a prisoner and he is concerned that the Ephesian Christians should not be discouraged by his sufferings. 'He is urging the Ephesian Christians not to faint at his tribulations for them, but rather to regard them as their own glory. In other words, what accounts for the digression is one of the most wonderful and moving things about the Apostle. We see here his great pastoral heart. His concern for others was his most outstanding characteristic' (D. M. Lloyd-Jones).

He encourages them by reminding them that though he is in a Roman prison, he is no prisoner of Rome but a prisoner of Jesus Christ (v.1). In other words, God is still in control of the situation. He uses the same sort of argument to the Philippians (1:12–18).

The prayer (3:14–21) for the Ephesians is prompted by the greatness of God's grace already shown to these Christians. But no matter how great the grace of God that we have experienced, there is always more. 'The apostle prayed that the saints might have a spiritual sight of Christ, a spiritual knowledge of Him, a spiritual enjoyment of Him, so that He would be present and precious to the soul; and that can only be by the exercise of faith in Him as He is revealed in the Scriptures. The apostle prayed for their hearts to be occupied with the excellency of His person, with His love and grace, with His blood and righteousness' (A. W. Pink).

The gospel does so many great things for us that Paul's application of it to the Christian is that we should live a life worthy of the grace of God. The remaining three chapters spell out very clearly what this means.

Notice the strength of the language in 4:17 – 'so I tell you this and insist on it in the Lord, that you must no longer live as the Gentiles do.' He is insisting that the great transformation indicated in chapter 2 be evidenced by a change of attitude and behaviour. The Christian is no longer in darkness, therefore he is to live as a child of the light (5:8). This means doing what pleases the Lord (5:10).

The Christian life is impossible without an experience of the great truths expounded in the first three chapters, but even then it is not easy and demands effort on our part. This effect is twofold. Firstly, it involves a putting off of the old self (4:22). We do this by rejecting the approaches of sin and by saying 'no' to it (4:25–31). We are not to wait for something to happen to us, we are to 'get rid of' sin. There is not to 'be even a hint' of sin in our lives. Secondly, we are to 'put on the new self' (4:24). This we do by promoting the fruit of light (5:9) in our lives. Paul works these things out in the specific relationships that most of us know: wives and husbands, children and parents, workers and employers.

The Christian life is not easy. In fact, it is a battle, and the great enemy, the devil, is ever vigorous in his opposition. So the Christian needs the armour of God (6:10–17). God supplies the armour but we are responsible for putting it on. Paul's teaching on the armour of God does not finish with verse 17; he immediately goes on to show us how vital prayer is in the battle. Even though prayer is not a part of the armour, it is indispensable to the success of the armour.

STUDY MATERIAL

Ephesians by Geoffrey Wilson (Banner of Truth, 1978).
Stand Firm: a young Christian's guide to the armour of God by Peter Jeffery (Evangelical Press of Wales, 1983).
There are eight volumes on Ephesians by Dr Lloyd-Jones. Each one is a gem (Banner of Truth).

∞ 15 ∞

Philippians

Philippi was a Roman colony in Macedonia in what we know today as northern Greece. 'It was Rome in miniature, a reproduction on a small scale of the imperial city' (W. Hendriksen). The church was founded there by Paul on his second missionary journey (Acts 16), about the year AD 50. It was the first city on the continent of Europe to hear the gospel.

Paul's first reception at Philippi was not a friendly one and he finished up in jail, but his relationship with the Philippian church was always cordial. The letter was written from prison in Rome about AD 61–63, and is warm in its gratitude for gifts sent (4:10–19) and in its expression of the apostle's love and concern for these Christians (1:3–8). 'What we have here is a genuine letter from Paul to his beloved church at Philippi. The writer passes from one subject to another just as we do today in writing to friends. (The difference is that Paul's letter is inspired; ours are not.) What holds these subjects together is not this or that central theme but the Spirit of God, mirrored forth, by means of a multitude of spiritual graces and virtues, in the heart of the apostle, proclaiming throughout that between God, the apostle, and the believers at Philippi there exists a blessed bond of glorious fellowship' (William Hendriksen).

CONTENTS

[78]

SUMMARY

Paul starts and ends this letter with grateful thanks to the Philippian Christians for their concern and love for him. He saw them as partners with him in the gospel (1:5), and they, feeling the same way, expressed their partnership in a very practical way (4:14–16). This gift, though apparently not desperately needed in the material sense (4:11), was of immense value in the spiritual uplift that it gave Paul (4:18) in a very difficult situation. 'The gift, after all, was valuable not so much for its own sake, as for what it indicated of affection and devotion in the givers. Paul could have done without the material aid, but he could not easily have done without the knowledge of true progress among his spiritual children' (J. Gresham Machen).

Paul was in prison at Rome but he sees even this as working to the advancement of the gospel (1:12). His confinement had been the means of encouraging many more Christians to speak out for the gospel (1:14). Motives may well have been wrong but the end product caused the heart of this man of God to rejoice (1:15–18). The first chapter is a great encouragement to Christians in difficult times. The source of the encouragement is the providence of God (1:6). This turns even adversity into blessing (1:12–18); it brings death into true focus (1:21–23); and it is the greatest possible incentive to Christian steadfastness even in the face of grave struggles (1:27–30).

In chapter 2 we have a thrilling description of the Lord Jesus Christ (2:6–11), and Paul gives us this in order to underline the need for Christian unity (2:2), and to show the only way in which it can be achieved. Being one in spirit and purpose is impossible if we allow 'selfish ambition and vain conceit' to infiltrate our fellowship. Therefore, our attitude should be Christlike. The humility which God demands from the Christian in 2:3 is seen clearly in the life of Jesus Christ (2:8).

Therefore (2:12), we are to live our lives without complaining or arguing and so shine in this dark world as true children of God (2:14–15). This should be the Christian's response to the life of obedience that we see in Christ. If our attitude is His attitude (2:5), then we will work out our salvation in such a way that we will shine like stars in a dark and sinful world.

This Christlikeness is seen in the lives of two Christians mentioned by Paul: Timothy and Epaphroditus (2:19–30). Timothy was not concerned for his own interest, but that of Christ, and Epaphroditus was willing to risk his life for his Saviour. Sadly, the same spirit is not seen in Euodia and Syntyche (4:2). These Christian women need help to sort out their differences and the other Christians at Philippi are urged to supply it (4:3).

Chapter 3 begins by exhorting us to rejoice in the Lord. This is repeated again in 4:4–5, with the added reminder that our gentleness is to be evident to all. But this does not mean that Christians turn a blind eye and show indifference to those who oppose the gospel. Paul speaks of these men as dogs (3:2) and enemies of the cross of Christ (3:18). 'There is here something bordering on fiery vehemence. But an incisive caution against a dangerous foe is not necessarily a sign of lovelessness. On the contrary, the warmer a father's affection for his son, the deeper will be his distress when that son's life is being persistently threatened by shrewd enemies, and the more will be his warnings. So it is also in the present instance. What Paul writes here in verse 2 is in complete harmony with the tender appellation in verse 1, where he addresses the members of the Philippian church as "my brothers"' (William Hendriksen).

These enemies are overcome and their false teaching will not affect the Christian if we, like Paul, have a high view of what it means to be a Christian (3:7–9) and have a hunger to know more and experience more of the Lord Jesus Christ (3:10–14). 'Our citizenship is in heaven' (3:20), therefore our minds need to be taken up with the things of God (4:8–9). We will never live like Christians until we learn to think like Christians, and we will never think like Christians until we spend more time with Christ. This means more prayer and more thanksgiving for blessings already ours (4:6).

STUDY MATERIAL

Philippians by Geoffrey Wilson (Banner of Truth, 1983).
The Message of Philippians by Alec Motyer (Inter-Varsity Press, 1984).

ᘒᘒ 16 ᘒᘒ

Colossians

The Lycus valley was about 100 miles east of Ephesus. In this valley were three towns which had Christian churches: Colossae, Laodicea and Hierapolis. These churches had not been founded by Paul. He had never met these believers personally (2:1) but nonetheless he is deeply concerned for them and writes with his usual warmth and passion.

The probability is that the Colossian church was founded by Epaphras (1:7), who was a native of the town (4:12). He was converted under Paul's preaching during a visit to Ephesus and had returned to his home-town to preach Christ to his fellow-Colossians. Paul's three years at Ephesus had been profitable, not only for the Ephesians but to the whole province of Asia (Acts 19:10). There must have been many like Epaphras who were converted at this time and subsequently took the gospel to cities that Paul could not visit.

The Colossian church was possibly established about AD 57. Some five years later while in prison in Rome, Paul heard of a problem of false teaching that was troubling this church, so he wrote this epistle to deal with what is known as the Colossian heresy. What exactly this heresy was is difficult to ascertain. 'One thing is clear – the false teachers insisted upon an ascetic manner of life, Col. 2.20–23. "Handle not, nor taste, nor touch" was their ordinance. Apparently they forbade the use of animal food and wine, Col. 2.16. There was also an excessive emphasis upon feast and fast days. The speculative side of their teaching, on the other hand, is obscure. It looks, however, as though they had inordinate reverence for angels, and boasted of higher mysteries to which they had attained. Whether the false teachers were Jews or Gentiles is uncertain. Colossians 2.11–15, which points out the

freedom of the Christian from the law and the superiority of
baptism over the rites of the Old Covenant, might seem to indicate
that the Colossians had been imbued with a false notion of the
continued validity of Judaism' (J. Gresham Machen).

The heresy is answered in a most positive and thrilling way by
exalting the Lord Jesus Christ as all-sufficient. There is therefore
no need for man's philosophy. Indeed, the supremacy of Christ as
set out by Paul in Colossians makes man's additions to the gospel
not only unnecessary but also ridiculous.

'In Christ all the fulness of the deity lives in bodily form' (2:9),
and something of that fulness is given to all Christians (2:10). 'The
parallels in Ephesians (1:23, 3:19) suggest the meaning that God
intends to flood the lives of men and women, and ultimately the
whole creation, with his own love, power and richness, and that he
has already begun to put this plan into effect through Christ and by
His Spirit. That is the Colossians' inheritance in Christ, and they
can want nothing more from any other source' (N. T. Wright).
Compared to this, how pathetic is a religion that is more concerned
with what to eat and drink (2:16) and all sorts of other man-made
rules (2:20–21).

CONTENTS

SUMMARY

While Paul writes this letter because of his concern over the
Colossian heresy he obviously has a very high regard for this
church (1:4–5). He is writing from prison in Rome but he is not at
all depressed by his own lack of freedom and the false teaching

[83]

attacking the churches. On the contrary, he rejoices 'that all over the world this gospel is producing fruit and growing' (1:6). Paul's prayer for the Colossians (1:9–14) is full of confidence, hope and joy.

Chapter 1:15–23 is a marvellous description of who the Lord Jesus Christ is and what He has done for us. Paul returns to the same glorious theme in 2:9–15, and it is no exaggeration for him to say, 'this is the Gospel' (1:23). 'All through the epistles of Paul, the life and death and resurrection are represented as events of a cosmic significance. But they can have such significance only if Christ is the kind of being that is described in the Epistle to the Colossians. The glorious account of salvation, which runs all through the epistles and forms the especial subject of the second group, is unintelligible if Christ were merely an inspired prophet or merely the greatest of created beings. It becomes intelligible only if Christ is "the image of the invisible God, the firstborn of all creation". The mysterious Christology of Colossians lies at the very heart of the Christian faith' (J. Gresham Machen).

Without doubt, the most effective answer to any heresy is the clear and bold proclamation of the person and work of Christ. Thus, the theme of Colossians is the pre-eminence of Christ, and how marvellously does Paul pursue this in 1:15–20 and 2:9–15! The concern that Paul has for the Colossians is very evident in 1:24–2:5. He prays and labours for them because he is concerned that they should be encouraged and united, and should benefit fully from all the riches of Christ (2:2). They are still young in the faith and he does not want them to be deceived by the false teachers' arguments that may sound fine but are in fact nothing more than the hollow, deceptive philosophies of men (2:4–8).

Paul gives us greater detail of this false teaching in 2:16–23. The details seem to show that the heresy contained a mixture of pagan rituals and Old Testament laws. Legalism (2:16), mysticism (2:18) and asceticism (2:21) may all have an appearance of wisdom about them (2:23) but they are of no value in the spiritual life. 'The gospel is fulness of life, free and without limit. For the gospel is Jesus Christ. Christ is the end of legalism for he is the end of the law (Rom. 10:4), in the sense that, by leading us to Jesus Christ, the law has achieved its purpose and also that those who are "in Christ" are no longer condemned by it (Rom. 8:1). Christ is the remedy for mysticism. Those who have found everything in Christ no longer need to seek other knowledge or experience elsewhere: Christ and his Word are completely sufficient. Christ is the negation of asceticism. His sacrifice is fully sufficient for our salvation, and trying to add any sacrifice of our own would be to challenge the power of the cross (Heb. 10:14). Let us, then, live fully and positively in the freedom and joy given by God, that is, in obedience to his Word and in the "friendship" of Jesus Christ (John 15:15)' (Guy Appere).

Freedom in Christ does not mean that we can live as we like. We are to live to please God. Thus, there is set before us a pattern of true Christian living (3:1–4:6). The morality of the New Testament is impossible without the doctrine of the New Testament. The false teaching said, 'If you do certain things, you will become a Christian.' The gospel says that it is the other way round. Only when you become a Christian can you live like a Christian. Dr Lloyd-Jones, commenting on the Sermon on the Mount, said, 'We are not told in the Sermon on the Mount, "Live like this and you will become Christian", rather we are told, "Because you are Christian live like this." This is how Christians ought to live; this is how Christians are meant to live.'

The last section of the epistle (4:7–18) is interesting in that it introduces us to several of Paul's fellow gospel workers. The apostle was no one-man band, he sought and needed, and certainly valued the help of people like Tychicus, Mark, Epaphras and Luke.

STUDY MATERIAL

Colossians by Geoffrey Wilson (Banner of Truth, 1980).
The Mystery of Christ – Meditations on Colossians by Guy Appéré (Evangelical Press, 1984).

∾ 17 ∾

The Thessalonian Epistles

Thessalonica was the capital city of the Roman province of Macedonia. Today we know the area as northern Greece and the city is still there but now it is called Thessaloniki. Paul had visited Thessalonica for a short period about AD 50 (Acts 17). The apostle was not there very long but his preaching was richly blessed by God. A few Jews were saved and also a 'large number of God-fearing Greeks' (Acts 17:4). These with the few prominent women made up the first Christian church in Thessalonica. They were mostly gentiles, people who had 'turned to God from idols' (1 Thess. 1:9).

The success of Paul's preaching resulted in the Jews becoming jealous and they stirred up serious trouble for God's servants (Acts 17:5–9). As a consequence of this, Paul had to flee from the city in the night. He had been there perhaps barely a month. 'He had not given his converts all the teaching which he felt was necessary to establish them securely in their new-found faith. He was leaving them to face a good deal of scoffing and petty persecution, if not indeed hostility of a more open and violent kind. They might well think that he had run away from the trouble which his coming had created, and left them in the lurch. He could not rest for thinking of them' (F. F. Bruce).

From Thessalonica Paul went via Berea and Athens to Corinth. He was deeply concerned for the infant church and he anxiously awaited news of how they were going on in the faith. This news came via Timothy (1 Thess. 3:6) while Paul was at Corinth. Almost immediately, Paul writes his first letter to these Christians. The date was about AD 51 and the epistle expresses the apostle's great relief and delight on hearing Timothy's news.

The second letter was written, again from Corinth, very soon

[86]

after the first. Apparently his teaching on the second coming of the Lord Jesus was being misunderstood at Thessalonica. So much so, that some Christians had even stopped working because they believed that the Lord's coming was so imminent (3:6–13). 'Accordingly Paul wrote the second letter as a sort of supplement to the first. Perhaps, before writing, he even read over again his rough draft of the former letter. At any rate, since his teaching was being misunderstood, it was natural for him to recall to his mind exactly what he had already said. That explains the similarity between the two epistles. In Second Thessalonians, parts of First Thessalonians are reiterated, with explanations and additions.

'The chief addition is the instruction about the second coming of Christ which is contained in 2 Thess. 2:1–12. In reply, Paul calls attention to certain elements in the oral teaching which he had given at the beginning. Christ will not come until "the lawless one" has been revealed' (Gresham Machen).

1 Thessalonians

CONTENTS

SUMMARY

In chapter 1 Paul remembers with obvious delight how the Thessalonians had responded to his preaching. Their conversion was so real that it was obvious to everyone, and consequently it was spoken of in Macedonia (northern Greece) and Achaia (southern Greece). The saving grace of the gospel is the result of the sovereign choice of God (v.4), the operation of the Holy Spirit upon the preached gospel (v.5), and the repentance and faith of the sinner (v.9).

Paul's sudden and early departure from Thessalonica was being used by the enemies of the gospel to attack his character and, by implication, the worth of the gospel that he preached. Paul answered this in 2:1–16 by explaining his conduct and by reminding the Thessalonians of what they know to be true. Notice how he says 'you knew' in verses 1, 5 and 11, and also 'you remember' (v.9) and 'you are witnesses' (v.10). 'What other people reported about the Thessalonians they themselves knew to be true. This opening shows Paul's confidence in his converts, and it also directs their attention to facts within their own knowledge that would refute the accusations of Paul's opponents. If the result of his preaching was so manifest and so definite, then clearly he could not have been the time-server he was now accused of being' (Leon Morris).

From 2:17 to 3:5 we see Paul's intense feeling for these immature Christians. He did not leave them, he was 'taken away'. And when he wanted to return to them, Satan prevented it. All this caused him deep anxiety and he was so concerned about them that when he 'could stand it no longer' (vv.1, 5), he sent Timothy to Thessalonica to obtain news. When Timothy returned with good news (3:6), Paul immediately writes this letter with all the warmth and passion, joy and delight of a man who truly cares and loves.

Having heard that they were going on well in the Christian faith, Paul now urges them to even greater commitment to the Lord in living a holy life. Thus in 4:1–12, he brings before them some crucial ingredients of holiness – control of one's sexual desires (vv.3–8); brotherly love (vv.9–10); and the conduct of one's daily activities (vv.11, 12).

The doctrine of the second coming of the Lord Jesus was causing some concern to these new Christians, mainly because they had misunderstood Paul's teaching on the subject. For instance, they were worried about Christians who had already died. Would they be at a disadvantage when Christ returned? The apostle seeks to put right their misunderstandings in 4:13–5:11. These words were meant to encourage them (4:18; 5:11).

The concluding verses, 5:12–28, contain seventeen pieces of sound spiritual advice on practical Christianity.

2 Thessalonians

CONTENTS

SUMMARY

The second letter begins very much in the same tone as the first, with Paul expressing his love and admiration for the Thessalonians (1:1–4). He then encourages them (1:5–10) that their suffering for Christ is not meaningless, and those who are causing them sorrow will ultimately be dealt with by God. He is reminding them of the coming day of judgement. Then with this in mind, the apostle assures these Christians that he is praying that on the day the Lord returns they will know the full blessing of Jesus being 'glorified in you and you in him' (1:11–12). 'This is not a prayer that the converts will not fall away. Paul's attention is fixed on the glory at the end time when he prays that they will then be adjudged worthy of having been called, i.e. that during the intervening period they will live in such a way as to ensure this commendation . . .' (Leon Morris).

In chapter 2 Paul comes to the reason he wrote this second letter. Some at Thessalonica were still confused about the Lord's second coming, and this was being aggravated by teaching, falsely attributed to Paul, which said that the day of the Lord had already come (2:2). As a result of believing this, some Christians had actually given up their jobs, seeing no purpose in working. Paul warns against this idleness (3:6–15).

The main thrust of Paul's argument (2:1–12) is not easy to interpret because Paul refers to teaching (v.5) of which we have no record. Nonetheless, it is clear that certain events must occur before the Lord returns (v.3). 'It is difficult to say who this man of lawlessness is, and there have been many suggestions, usually some outstanding evil person at the time of the suggestion. Throughout history there have been many who have done Satan's evil work (cf. the "many antichrists", 1 John 2:18) and this is a warning against over-hasty identification of the man of this chapter with any historical personage. Paul's concern is not with the evil ones who appear from time to time, but with the most infamous of all, one who will appear in the last days. He never uses the term "Antichrist", but plainly he has in mind the being John calls by this name. He is not Satan, for he is distinguished from him (v.9); but he is Satan's instrument, imbued with Satan's spirit' (Leon Morris).

This man of lawlessness has not yet come but when he does appear, he will be thoroughly defeated by the Lord Jesus Christ (v.8). His followers will perish (v.10). These are compared to the Thessalonian Christians (2:13–17), who are loved by the Lord and will share in the glory of Christ.

Finally, Paul asks for prayer (3:1–5). He has great confidence in God in spite of all the opposition, and rests in the faithfulness of his Saviour.

STUDY MATERIAL

1 & 2 Thessalonians by Geoffrey Wilson (Banner of Truth, 1982).
1 & 2 Thessalonians by Leon Morris (Inter-Varsity Press, 1984).

☙ 18 ☙

The Pastoral Epistles

First and Second Timothy and Titus were written during a period that is not covered by the Acts. Acts closes in AD 63 with Paul in prison in Rome, but it is highly likely that he was released and had a few more years of missionary work.

During these years Paul wrote 1 Timothy and Titus, about AD 66–67. He was then re-arrested and imprisoned in Rome, not under house arrest this time but in a dungeon, and from there he wrote 2 Timothy shortly before he died.

Timothy was converted as a young man during Paul's first visit to Lystra. His father was a Greek and his mother a Jewess. When Paul visited Lystra again (Acts 16:1–3), Timothy joined him in his ministry.

Paul writes these two letters to Timothy when the younger man was at Ephesus. There he had no easy task (1 Tim. 1:3) and the apostle writes to encourage him and to advise him on how to cope as the leader of a Christian church.

Titus was one of Paul's most faithful and trusted helpers. He is not mentioned in Acts but there are several references to his ministry in the epistles. When Paul writes to him he was at Crete, facing a very similar problem as Timothy at Ephesus. So the apostle writes to these two men to help them in their difficulties as Christian leaders. The letters are private, but are also meant for all God's people. 'These Epistles are not merely private letters. Though addressed to individuals among Paul's friends, they are addressed to them not as individuals, but rather as leaders in the Church. From the first they were intended to be read not by Timothy and Titus alone, but also by the churches over which these men were placed. With some justice they may be called "Pastoral Epistles"; in them Timothy and Titus are addressed in their capacity as pastors. The Pastoral Epistles are – if the word be properly understood – "official" communications' (J. Gresham Machen).

The churches were now about ten years old. They were growing and needed some organisation and structure. In the pastoral epistles these vital issues were dealt with.

1 Timothy

CONTENTS

1:1–3	Greetings
4–11	False teachers at Ephesus
12–20	God's goodness to Paul
2:1–15	Public worship and the place of women in it
3:1–16	Qualifications for church leaders
4:1–16	False teachers and how Timothy is to deal with them
5:1–6:2	Instructions for various groups in the church
6:3–21	Money and true riches

SUMMARY

Paul tells us plainly why he wrote this letter in chapter 3, verses 14 and 15. It was that Timothy might know how people ought to behave in God's church. By the church, Paul does not mean the building but the people. So he is referring to how we as Christians relate to each other, and to our place among God's people. We cannot do as we see fit, there is a proper way to behave. And this is so because it is God's church.

The head of the church is not the queen, nor the pope, nor the minister; the head is God. We are told in this letter many things about God:

1:17	He is the only God and eternal
6:15	He is King of kings and Lord of lords

Paul delights in God as immortal (1:17; 6:16); invisible (1:17; 6:16) and incarnate (3:16).

[92]

The church of God consists of men and women who were sinners but who have now repented of their sin and come in faith to Jesus for salvation (1:13–16; 2:3, 6). The church consists of sinners saved by grace, but they are still sinners, not perfect people. Therefore, their behaviour will not always be what it ought to be. So God needs to tell us how to behave (3:14–15) and also give us leaders to teach us these things.

In chapter 3, we are shown the qualifications for these leaders. In the New Testament, overseer, bishop and elder all refer to the same office. Basically, the church has two forms of leadership: elders and deacons. The clear biblical norm is that leaders are to lead, not to accommodate the whims of the people. Note that Timothy is told to command: 1:3; 4:11 and 6:17–18. But our fallen human nature is such that people do not like being commanded and so those doing the commanding can expect criticism. For this, as well as for other reasons, there are certain qualities in leaders that are essential. For instance, an elder (3:3) must not be violent, but gentle, not quarrelsome. Clearly, if elders were to react in the same way as they are often treated, there would be civil war in the church.

There are several references to false teaching (1:3–7; 4:1–8; 6:3–5). We are told two things about false doctrine: its origin is the devil (4:1), and it is to be recognized by its lack of conformity to the glorious gospel (1:11). Sometimes true believers are deceived by these teachings and they must be warned (4:6) and pleaded with in love (1:5).

Paul has much to say to Timothy about the place of women in the church (2:9–15; 5:3–16). We need to remind ourselves that these are not the opinions of a crusty old bachelor with a bias against women; they are part of the inspired Word of God. The apostle shows a great concern for the needs of women, and mentions widows in particular (5:3–16). The church has a responsibility to help meet the needs of these ladies.

All these things – the greatness of God, the fact that Christians are sinners saved by grace, the value of leadership, the evil of false teaching, the place of women in the church and the care that the church is to exercise towards those in need – all these are dealt with as Paul tells us how to conduct ourselves in church.

Lastly, Paul deals with the Christian and money (6:3–19). He warns us that: 'The desire to become rich causes the man . . . to fall into numerous cravings. One kind of craving easily leads to another.

The person who craves riches generally also yearns for honour, popularity, power, ease, the satisfaction of the desires of the flesh etc. All spring from the same root, selfishness, which, being the worst possible method of really satisfying the "self", is both senseless and hurtful' (William Hendriksen).

2 Timothy

CONTENTS

SUMMARY

This is the last of Paul's letters, written shortly before his death during his second imprisonment at Rome. He was not now, as during his first Roman imprisonment, in the relative comfort of the hired house but in some 'dismal underground dungeon with a hole in the ceiling for light and air' (William Hendriksen). He was in chains (1:16; 2:9). It seems from 1:17 that the Christians in Rome did not know where the apostle was imprisoned. It was very difficult and lonely for Paul (4:16), but he is not in despair and his chief concern is for the future of the gospel. 'We are to imagine the apostle, "Paul the aged", languishing in some dark, dank dungeon in Rome, from which there is to be no escape but death. His own apostolic labours are over. "I have finished the race," he can say. But now he must make provision for the faith after he has gone, and especially for its transmission (uncontaminated, unalloyed) to future generations. So he sends Timothy this most solemn charge. He is to preserve what he has received, at whatever cost, and to hand it on to faithful men who in their turn will be able to teach others also (2:2)' (John Stott).

In chapter 1, Timothy is encouraged to remain faithful to the gospel. The gospel needs to be guarded (1:14). This is too great a task for any man but the help of the Holy Spirit is promised. Paul encourages Timothy, reminding him of the faithfulness of his mother and grandmother (1:5) and giving him his own testimony (1:11, 12).

The best way to guard and preserve the gospel is to preach it. In chapter 2, Timothy is exhorted to do this (vv.2, 14, 24), but this will not be easy. It requires the endurance of a soldier (v.3), the dedication and discipline of an athlete (v.5), and the hard work of a farmer (v.6). Even then, personal suffering may well be the outcome (v.9). The gospel needs to be guarded because of the false versions of it that abound (vv.14–18). Timothy is called upon to handle the Word of God in such a way as will meet with God's approval (v.15). 'The man who handles the word of truth properly does not change, pervert, mutilate or distort it, neither does he use it with a wrong purpose in mind. On the contrary, he prayerfully interprets Scripture in the light of Scripture. He courageously, yet lovingly, applies its glorious meaning to concrete conditions and circumstances, doing this for the glory of God, the conversion of sinners, and the edification of believers' (William Hendriksen).

Opposition to the gospel never wavers (3:1–8). This fact, coupled with the stark reality of 3:12, 13, could have been very depressing for a young pastor like Timothy. Paul does not encourage Timothy with prospects of an easy life. He repeats the same truths in 4:3, 4. But over and against these dark warnings, there is the absolute confidence in the victory of the gospel. Timothy needs to know that these evil men will not triumph:

3:9	they will not get very far
3:10	the Lord rescued me from all of them
4:7–8	the ultimate triumph

'Our God is the God of history. "God is working his purpose out, as year succeeds to year." "He buries his workmen, but carries on his work." The torch of the Gospel is handed down by each generation to the next. As leaders of the former generation die, it is all the more urgent for those of the next generation to step forward bravely to take their place. Timothy's heart must have been profoundly moved by this exhortation from Paul the old warrior who had led him to Christ. We cannot rest for ever on the leadership of the preceding generation. The day comes when we must step into their shoes and ourselves take the lead. That day had come for Timothy. It comes to all of us in time . . .

'So then, in view of the coming of Christ to judgment, of the contemporary world's distaste for the Gospel and of the imprisoned apostle's imminent death, the latter's charge to Timothy had a note of solemn urgency: Preach the word!' (John R. W. Stott).

Titus

CONTENTS

SUMMARY

Paul thought a great deal of Titus and three times he sent him to Corinth on difficult pastoral work. Crete was another church with serious problems and Titus is entrusted by the apostle to deal with these (1:5). The people of Crete did not have a very good reputation (1:12) and Paul agrees with this assessment (1:13). From among this type of people, men and women had been converted and a church formed. Unfortunately, some of these national characteristics were still evident even in people who were now Christians and this was inflamed by 'those of the circumcision group', that is, Jewish Cretans who had professed faith in Christ. These were being influenced by non-Christian Jews (vv.14–16).

These rebellious church members must be silenced (1:11) and Paul instructs Titus to do two things in order to accomplish this. The first is to appoint elders (1:5). This will have the effect of letting everyone know who the true leaders of the church are and thus frustrate false claims of leadership. And if these elders are the sort of men described in vv.6–9, they will be able 'to encourage others by sound doctrine and refute those who oppose it.'

Secondly, Titus himself is to teach sound doctrine (2:1) or to be more accurate, he is to teach what is in accord and consistent with sound doctrine. Only biblical doctrine produces a Christian life that pleases God. Note the comparison with what the Cretans were by nature (1:12) and what they are to be by grace (2:11–12). This section (2:1–3:14) takes up most of the epistle. Paul's great concern is that 'our people' (3:14) should learn how to live useful lives and not act as they had previously acted (3:3). So the practical side of Christianity is taught clearly.

But still, there are some very rich doctrinal passages in Titus that glory in the gospel: 2:11–14; 3:4–7.

STUDY MATERIAL

Pastoral Epistles by Geoffrey Wilson (Banner of Truth, 1982).
The Message of 2 Timothy by John Stott (Inter-Varsity Press, 1973).

๑ 19 ๑

Philemon

This letter was written by Paul from Rome at the same time that he wrote to the Colossians, about AD 62. The apostle must have written many personal letters to friends and converts, but this is the only one that has survived.

Philemon was a rich Christian and a member of the church at Colossae. Onesimus was one of his slaves who had escaped and apparently stolen some money (v.18) in the process. He had made his way to Rome, where in the providence of God, he came into contact with Paul and was converted.

Onesimus is now a Christian, and Paul believes that it is right for him to return to his master and put right any wrongs that he had done. So Paul sends him back to Philemon with this letter. Both Philemon (v.19) and Onesimus (v.10) came to faith under Paul's ministry, so he is superbly qualified to act as a go-between. The letter is written with great tact as he pleads for the erring slave.

CONTENTS

SUMMARY

Paul does not open this letter, as he does most others, by referring to himself as an apostle. Rather, he refers to himself as a prisoner of Christ. This he does several times: in v.1, vv.9–10, v.13 and v.23. 'The mention of himself as a prisoner of Christ Jesus is also very tactful, probably implying, In comparison with the sacrifice that I am making is not the favor which I am asking you to grant a rather easy matter?' (William Hendriksen).

Philemon is described by Paul as a dear friend, and he obviously has a very high opinion of this man. His reputation for generosity and kindness to God's people was well known (vv.4–7). Because of this, Paul feels confident as he makes his plea for Onesimus (v.20).

When Onesimus was a slave previously, he had been useless to Philemon because of a grudging service but now he is useful (v.11). The name Onesimus means 'useful' and Paul argues this man can now really live up to his name because he is a new creature in Christ.

So the running away of this slave, under the providence of God (vv.15–16), has worked out for the good of Philemon. Paul pleads therefore that Onesimus should not be received harshly as runaway slaves normally were, but as a brother in Christ.

STUDY MATERIAL

Colossians and Philemon by Geoffrey Wilson (Banner of Truth, 1980).
The Message of Colossians and Philemon by R. C. Lucas (Inter-Varsity Press, 1980).

⁀ 20 ⁀

Hebrews

Hebrews is introduced in the Authorized Version of the Bible as 'the Epistle of Paul to the Hebrews'. These words are not part of the original writings and today very few evangelical scholars would accept that Paul was the author. Though he may have written it, its authorship is very doubtful. This is not just the view of modern evangelicals. John Calvin in the 16th century said, 'I can adduce no reason to show that Paul was its author'. Writing in 1537, Martin Luther suggested that Apollos was the author. To be fair, one has to acknowledge that the Puritan, John Owen, and the modern writer, A. W. Pink, come down very firmly in favour of Paul as the writer of Hebrews.

We will never know, and it does not really matter. Hebrews is part of the inspired Word of God and its authority is not derived from any human author but from its divine origins. It was probably written sometime between AD 65 and AD 70, to a group of Jewish Christians who were being tempted to regret becoming Christians. They had stood firm in the face of early persecutions (10:32–34) but this had weakened their resolve. 'They were men of some intellectual ability. The group had been established a good many years (2:3; 13:7), and had a history of persecution. They should have been mature Christians by this time, capable of teaching others (5:11–6:2). Instead they are withdrawn and inward looking. And they seem to have half a mind to turn back to Judaism. They need a forceful reminder that what they possess in Christ is far better' (*The Lion Handbook*).

These people needed two things – a warning and an encouragement – and both are here in Hebrews. The most severe warnings against turning their back on the faith are found in 6:4–8, 10:26–31 and 12:25. Yet there is also the great encouragement of the superiority of Christianity to their old Judaism. Christ Himself is superior to angels (1:4); far greater than Moses (3:3); and in Christianity there is a better covenant and better promises (8:6); there are better sacrifices (9:23) and a better hope (7:19). These are reasons enough in difficult times to 'hold on' (3:6); 'make every effort' (4:11); 'hold firmly' (4:14); 'go on to maturity' (6:1); and to be 'greatly encouraged' (6:18).

'Although deeply aware of the problems these believers are facing, the author of this letter does not turn to his necessary pastoral exhortation until he has first reminded them of the uniqueness of Christ. He presents them first of all with an exposition of Christ as prophet (1:1–2), priest (1:3b) and king (1:8–14). Some of their Christian friends had slipped back into Judaism. They had placed their trust not in the work of Christ, but in the works of the law. They had abandoned their faith not only because it was too costly for them to continue, but because they had an inadequate understanding of Christ in the first place. Many of our contemporaries are fascinated by Jesus. We have rock-musicals which present us with an interpretation of Christ's teaching and mission. Commercial films, radio plays and television presentations invite us to look at Christ. But is their portraiture adequate? Nothing is of greater importance in our own time than a reminder of the immense dimensions of the biblical doctrine of Christ' (Raymond Brown).

CONTENTS

SUMMARY

The letter was written to Jewish Christians who were being persecuted for their faith by non-Christian Jews. As a consequence, they were beginning to wonder if it was worth being a Christian. They missed the splendour and grandeur of the temple ceremonies and the comfort of visible religious objects. Added to this, they had believed that Jesus was to come again, but now it was over 30 years since the ascension and still there had been no second coming. So they had all sorts of spiritual problems. Doubts, regrets and confusion abounded. How are these to be counteracted? By showing the supreme and unique authority of the Lord Jesus Christ.

The first verse immediately reminds us of one of the greatest facts of our faith – 'God spoke'. This takes Christianity out of the realm of mere human speculation and opinion. Its authority is that God spoke. How? Not through subjective feelings or odd impulses but through the prophets. In other words, through the Old Testament Scriptures. So what these Jewish Christians had before they became Christians was divinely inspired. Why, then, leave it and come to Christ? Because whilst the Old Testament is true, it does not contain all the truth. The final and complete truth is in Christ. To underline this, we are shown the glory and uniqueness of Christ. Verse 3 of chapter 1 is a magnificent description of Jesus. 'The whole revelation and manifestation of God is now in Christ; He alone reveals the Father's heart. It is not only that Christ declared or delivered God's message, but that He Himself was and is God's message. All that God has to say to us is in His Son: all His thoughts, counsels, promises, gifts, are to be found in the Lord Jesus' (A. W. Pink).

After such an opening, almost anything would be an anticlimax, but the superiority of Jesus over prophets, angels and even Moses is stressed, culminating with the warning of 4:1–13. The Israelites of the Old Testament rebelled against the leadership of Moses and brought upon themselves the wrath and judgement of God (3:16–19). These first-century Jewish Christians must be careful that the same thing does not happen to them – but it will if the gospel that they have heard and believed is not lived out in faith (4:2). They must work at their faith, not let difficulties beat them, and make every effort (4:11) to obtain all that God has for us in Christ. 'Christian pilgrims in the contemporary world must realize that, in the light of a passage such as this, it will not do to confess a merely nominal allegiance to Christian truth or pay occasional lip service in meetings and services to faith in Christ.

Our commitment must be sincere and genuine' (Raymond Brown).

It is one thing to tell a depressed Christian to make every effort, but how do you actually get him to do it? Hebrews deals with this problem in two ways. Firstly, by encouragement and, secondly, by a severe warning. The encouragement is spelt out clearly in 4:14–16. We are not left to ourselves in this. Great and superior though Christ is, He knows exactly how we feel when we are tempted, and He is very approachable. If that is so, why don't we come to Him? The answer is ignorance (5:11–14) and spiritual immaturity, which is the result of laziness (6:12). The word 'slow' in 5:11 is the same word as 'lazy' in 6:12. When we feel sorry for ourselves, the tendency is to neglect prayer and Scripture. This laziness is deadly and deepens rather than helps the spiritual problem.

The warnings of 6:1–12 and 10:19–39 have caused some Christians great problems because they appear to teach that it is possible to fall from grace and lose your salvation. Dr Martyn Lloyd-Jones, after examining the various terms used to describe the people under consideration in these passages, reaches the following conclusion:

'Thus we have looked at the particular terms of these statements in Hebrews, chapter 6 and 10. The important thing to notice is that all these terms taken together have a definite limit to them. Nowhere are we told that these people were "born again", that they were regenerate; nowhere are we told that they have been justified; nowhere are we told that they have been sanctified; nowhere are we told that they have been sealed by the Spirit; nowhere are we told that they have been adopted into God's family. I emphasize this for the reason that when references are made to true believers it is always the case that the terms "justified" and "sanctified" and so on, are used . . . What we are told about these people is not that they are regenerate, not that they are justified, not that they are reconciled to God; but they have certain experiences which had brought them into the Church and made them think, and made everyone else think, that they were truly Christian. They had claimed to believe the truth; they had some remarkable experiences in the realm of the Church together with others, some indeed may even have had some of the miraculous gifts. But all that does not necessarily

prove that a man is a Christian, that he is regenerate'
(D. M. Lloyd-Jones).

These passages in chapters 6 and 10 put before us a terrible
possibility – not that true believers can lose their salvation, but that
it is possible for a person to have certain resemblances to a Christian,
suppose that he is a Christian, and yet not be saved. The writer to the
Hebrews does not intend true Christians to doubt their salvation.
He goes on to say in 6:9, 'Even though we speak like this, dear
friends, we are confident of better things in your case – things that
accompany salvation'. The words 'in your case' mean that 6:4–6
does not refer to the Jewish Christians that he is writing to. Though
'he had spoken it unto them, he did not speak it of them' (John
Owen). Far from teaching 'falling from grace', Hebrews 6 goes on to
teach in no uncertain terms the eternal security of all believers. Read
verses 17–20. Dr P. E. Hughes writes of these verses: 'The
personal security of the man whose hope rests on Christ is intended.
The metaphor of an anchor in itself effectively portrays the concept
of fixity, for the function of an anchor is to provide security in the
face of changing tides and rising storms. Human anchors cannot
hold man's life secure in the stresses and troubles that assail it; but
the anchor of Christian hope is unfailingly sure and steadfast. There
is an immense contrast between the former restless and meaningless
existence which those who have "Fled for refuge" (verse 18) have
left behind them and the stability which, through fixing their
confidence in Christ, they now enjoy.'

Melchizedek was mentioned in 5:10, then again in 6:20, and on
both occasions we are told that Jesus was a priest after the order of
Melchizedek. Chapter 7 now tells us what this means. Do not
forget the reason for this epistle. These Hebrew Christians were
wavering in their faith and looking back longingly at their old
Judaism with its high priest and sacrifices. In their confused state,
they were forgetting the limitations of the Levitical priesthood.
These limitations are listed:

7:23	priests died and had to be replaced
7:27–28	priests were sinners
10:11	the sacrifices needed to be repeated

All the priests had to be of the tribe of Levi (7:5) but Jesus was
from the tribe of Judah, so how could He be a priest? The Levitical
priests were of the order of Aaron (7:11). ('Order' here means line

or descendants of Aaron.) The answer is that Jesus was of the order of Melchizedek. Chapter 7:1–10 refers to the happenings of Genesis 14. Melchizedek was king as well as priest, and the Genesis 14 incident proved he was superior to the Levites (7:6–10). More than this, Melchizedek was unique (7:3). 'Unlike the Levitical priests, the priesthood of Melchizedec was not limited to a prescribed period nor did it depend for its exercise upon a carefully preserved genealogy, for his priestly office was derived from his personal dignity, and in this he resembled the Son of God. The immeasurable superiority of Christ's Priesthood over the earthly order which it replaced rests upon the divine dignity of his eternal Sonship' (Geoffrey B. Wilson).

The limitations of the old priesthood are not to be found in the priesthood of Jesus:

7:23–25	Jesus lives forever
7:26	Jesus is sinless
10:10–14	No more sacrifices are needed

Chapter 8 develops the theme of the superiority of the priesthood of Jesus and the superiority of the new covenant that Jesus has established between God and His people. In Exodus 24, 'We have a description of the inauguration of the covenant between the Lord and the people of the Lord. By it they became the people of the Lord, they came to stand in a special relationship to God. The covenant is that on which all the rest stands. The whole system of worship, for example, was that for the people in covenant relationship to God. The laws were the laws for the maintenance of the covenant. It is not too much to say that the thought of the covenant dominated the thinking of the men of the Old Testament. For them it was of supreme importance that they stood in such a relation to the Lord as did no other people' (Leon Morris).

Both the old and new covenants are the provision of God for His people, helpless in the grip of sin. The difference between them is the person and work of Christ. Whilst the old covenant looks forward to, and anticipates Christ, the new celebrates His coming and on-going ministry. The old covenant is now obsolete (8:13) and it is replaced by a new and better covenant. The reason why the new is better is worked out in chapter 9. Notice two important verses, 11 and 24. See the emphasis they lay on our Lord. They begin, 'When Christ . . .' and 'For Christ . . .'. In this way, the writer of the letter shows how Jesus surpasses and perfects all that Aaron stood for. To the Son of God and His work, words like 'greater', 'more perfect' (v.11), 'how much more' (v.14) and 'better' (v.23) are applied.

Many points of contrast are suggested here. Consider especially the following:

The priests offered the blood of animals (v.13): Christ offered His own (vv.14, 26).

The high priest entered the most holy place in the tabernacle (v.7): Christ entered heaven (v.24).

The priests dealt only in patterns, representations, symbols (v.23): Christ goes beyond these to the true and the real (v.24).

The high priests knew no rest from their labours; their service was constantly repeated, and therefore incomplete: Christ's sacrifice was complete and final (v.26).

It must be remembered that chapter 9 does not set out to show how God 'tried' the Old Testament method, and then, when it failed, sent Christ instead. The Old Testament sacrifices accomplished admirably what they were intended to do, which was to point to Him who alone could 'bear the sins of many'. All this is meant to encourage these depressed Christians to 'draw near to God with a sincere heart in full assurance of faith' (10:22). Further encouragement is given in chapter 11 in the examples of faith of great men and women of the past. These folk did not have an easy time (11:35–38) but they kept their eyes on God. Therefore (12:1) with such examples the Hebrew Christians are urged to fix their eyes on Jesus (12:2). Only in this way will their feeble arms and weak knees be strengthened (12:12). The book concludes with more warnings, encouragements and exhortations.

What greater encouragement could there be for dejected believers than the promise of 13:5 – 'Never will I leave you: never will I forsake you'? This quotation being true, we as Christians can with every confidence apply to ourselves the words of Psalm 118:6,7 – 'The Lord is my helper: I will not be afraid. What can man do to me?'

STUDY MATERIAL

Hebrews by Geoffrey Wilson (Banner of Truth, 1970).
The Message of Hebrews by Raymond Brown (Inter-Varsity Press, 1982).

ॐ 21 ॐ

James

We are told in the first verse of the letter that it was written by James. But which James? There are three important men in the New Testament who bear the name James. They are James the son of Zebedee, James the son of Alphaeus and James the brother of the Lord Jesus. Traditionally, the authorship has been ascribed to James the Lord's brother. 'He was not, indeed, one of the twelve apostles, and during the earthly life of Jesus was not even a believer at all, John 7:5. But having been granted a special appearance of the risen Lord, 1 Cor. 15:7, and having united himself with the little company of apostles and faithful women who were waiting for the coming of the Spirit, Acts 1:14, he became afterwards the leader of the Jerusalem church, Acts 12.17; 15:4–29; Gal.2:9; Acts 21:18' (J. Gresham Machen).

The letter was written to Jewish Christians living outside Palestine (1:2). These people had accepted Jesus as the Messiah, but their conduct did not match their doctrine. So James says very little about doctrine but much about the danger of 'faith' without works. 'His purpose is clearly not so much to inform, but to command, exhort and encourage. Yet James issues his commands, for the most part, in a tone of tender pastoral concern, addressing his readers fifteen times as "my brothers" or "my beloved brothers"' (Douglas J. Moo).

Though he is tender, James is not soft and he leaves his readers in no doubt as to what he thinks in language that is uncompromising (2:20; 3:9, 10; 4:4). Some people have thought that there is a contradiction between James and Paul on the doctrine of justification, and this may seem to be so from 2:20–24.

Because of this, Martin Luther went so far as to call James an epistle of straw. The problem is not so great if we remember that James and Paul were seeking to answer two different questions. Paul was asking, How do we obtain salvation? And the answer is clear – not by our own efforts but by faith in Christ. James was asking, What is the proof that we are truly saved? And his answer is equally clear – by the fruit it produces in the Christian's life. To say that you have faith and for that faith not to govern how you live is in effect a denial of faith.

'According to James, faith without works is dead; according to Paul, faith is all-sufficient for salvation. But what does James mean by faith? The answer is perfectly plain. The faith which James is condemning is a mere intellectual assent which has no effect upon conduct. The demons also, he says, have that sort of faith, and yet evidently they are not saved, James 2:19.

What Paul means by faith is something entirely different; it is not a mere intellectual assent to certain propositions, but an attitude of the entire man by which the whole life is entrusted to Christ. In other words, the faith that James is condemning is not the faith that Paul is commending' (J. Gresham Machen).

CONTENTS

SUMMARY

James is intensely concerned with the practical outworking of the Christian faith in the lives of all God's people. His whole message can be summed up in the words of 1:22, 'Do not merely listen to the word . . . Do what it says.' If we listen to the Word of God but do not obey it, we deceive ourselves into thinking that we are Christian when in reality we are not (1:26). Such self-deception may be accompanied by much talk about faith (2:14–26), but a faith that does not show itself in actions is useless. Indeed, it is not what the Bible means by faith. Dead faith is no faith. Living a life of obedience to the Word of God is not easy. Trials and temptations war against the Christian to restrict obedience, therefore perseverance is needed (1:2–18). Poverty or riches bring their own problems (1:9–12), but whatever the temptation, it is not God who sends it. Temptation is the consequence of a sinful human nature, but it can be overcome (read and memorise 1 Corinthians 10:13). The answer to temptation is to know and apply the Word of God to every situation that confronts us. This, James urges us to do (1:21–25) because this is how our Saviour dealt with temptation (Luke 4:1–13).

The temptation to show favouritism is a very real one in any church fellowship (2:1–7). 'James' illustration is timeless. It speaks as loudly today as when he penned it. It is still not always easy to know how to accommodate a tramp in a worship-service and it still is easy to assume that wealth gives a commanding voice in church affairs. The sin of partiality is the sin of judging by accidents and externals and, as James noted, it always bears down on the poor and disadvantaged' (Alec Motyer).

Once again, James reminds us that the answer to this is a correct application of the direction of Scripture (2:8–11). A faith which ignores what God says in his Word is fruitless, and James asks the penetrating question, 'Can such a faith save?' Such faith is useless and dead and bears no resemblance to the true faith that we read of in the lives of great men of Scripture like Abraham.

James then moves on to deal with the tongue. He insists upon the importance of the controlled tongue because it is a key factor in all we do. Two illustrations are used to make this point – the bit in the horse's mouth (3:3) and the rudder of a ship (3:4). The language of 3:5, 6 is very strong but it is not inappropriate because the potential for sin that lies in the tongue is frightening. How we need wisdom that does not originate in us, but comes to us from heaven (3:13–18). Such a wisdom is available to us from God (1:5).

Wisdom produces peacemakers. This is in stark contrast to the strife and worldliness described in chapter 4. Centuries before in the Old Testament, Job said, 'the fear of the Lord – that is wisdom, and to shun evil is understanding' (28:28). In this chapter, James is saying the same thing. The activities described are a result of not fearing God. James says it is hatred of God (4:4). He calls us to shun evil (4:7–10) and come back to God, a God who is full of compassion and mercy (5:11). Being a Christian is not easy; that is why James commences his letter urging perseverance. He concludes by exhorting his readers to be patient (5:7). Job is given to us as an example (5:11) of patience, and then Elijah is brought before us as an example of prayer. In case we be tempted to excuse ourselves by pleading that these were very special men and we could never be like them, James makes the point that 'Elijah was a man just like us'. He feared, got depressed, felt like packing everything in, and ran away – but look how God used him (5:17–18).

STUDY MATERIAL

The Message of James by Alec Motyer (Inter-Varsity Press, 1985).
Truth for Life by John Blanchard (Evangelical Press, 1986).

1 Peter

Peter wrote this letter about AD 64–65 to Christians in Pontus, Galatia, Cappadocia, Asia and Bithynia (1:1). The churches in these areas would have been mixed congregations of Jews and gentiles. It was written from Babylon (5:13). It is almost certain that this does not refer to the ancient city of Babylon in Mesopotamia. Peter is probably using the name 'Babylon' as it is used elsewhere in the New Testament as a reference to Rome (Rev. 16:19; 17:5; 18:2). In the Old Testament, Babylon was representative of the world's power in opposition to God, and in the New Testament, Rome was the equivalent.

Peter writes to encourage Christians who were facing difficult times (5:12). There are several references to suffering in this letter, which is written with a warm pastoral concern. 'The letter is full of encouragement and witness common to the apostolic teaching; we may assume that this is not the first time that Peter has taught these things. But the letter is freely written; Peter does not piece together material drawn from others. He speaks with deep understanding and feeling, out of his own knowledge as an apostle of Christ' (Edmund P. Clowney).

This is only a brief letter but it covers an astonishing breadth of ground. 'In only 105 verses, 1 Peter ranges over a wide field of Christian theology and ethics. Here is the great doctrine of redemption, from its conception before the foundation of the world to its consummation in our receiving an inheritance that will never fade away. Here are repeated calls to holiness and to humble trust in God for each day's needs. Here is practical counsel – for marriage, for work, for relating to the government, for witnessing to unbelievers, for using spiritual gifts, for serving as a church officer' (Wayne Grudem).

There are many quotations from the Old Testament but no direct quotations from Jesus; nevertheless, Peter is continually alluding to the Saviour's teaching.

For example, compare the Sermon on the Mount with 1 Peter:

on persecution   Matt. 5:10–11 and 1 Pet. 3.14
on good deeds   Matt. 5:16 and 1 Pet. 2:12
on the Christian's inheritance   Matt. 6:19–21 and 1 Pet. 1:4

CONTENTS

SUMMARY

In the first chapter, Peter reminds his readers of the great privilege of being a Christian. The Christian is chosen (v.2), born again (v.3), has a great inheritance (v.4), is shielded by God's power (v.5) and brought into a living and precious relationship with Jesus Christ (v.8). None of this is of our doing but of the grace and mercy of God and purchased for us at great cost (vv.18–19).

The implication of this is twofold. Firstly, it puts present suffering into a proper context (vv.7, 8), and secondly, it brings upon the Christian the obligation to seek to be holy (vv.13–16). These two things are very closely related, both in the first century and now. 'The readers of First Peter were tempted to relinquish what was distinctive in their faith in order to avoid the hostility of their heathen neighbours; we are tempted to do the same thing because the superficial respectability of modern life has put a gloss of polite convention over the profound differences that divide the inner lives of men. We, as well as the first readers of the Epistle, need to be told that this world is lost in sin, that the blood of Christ has ransomed an elect race from the city of destruction, that the high privileges of the Christian calling demand spotless purity and unswerving courage' (J. Gresham Machen).

The suffering that Peter has in mind is not that of sickness or poor health but rather the opposition of the world to a Christian simply because he is Christian. The Christian life-style is so different from the world's that it creates hostility (2:12). This should not surprise us (4:12), for it is exactly what happened to our Lord Jesus Christ (2:21–22). The important thing is that our suffering is for doing good, not for doing evil (3:14–17; 4:14–19), so that we do not lash out at our attackers (3:9). We are to follow the example set by Jesus (2:23).

All this sounds very praiseworthy, but how possible is it? It is only possible if we take 1:13–16 seriously. Here is a real Christianity in action and it is the result of a living relationship with Christ. This is not a lifeless, formal religion, but one vibrating with experience and reality. Peter describes it in 1:8 and 2:4–10. 'Peter had seen Jesus, and loved him. Does it amaze him that distant and scattered Gentiles who have never seen Jesus also know and love him? Peter well knows that it is not his physical association with Jesus that joins him to his Saviour. He knows Jesus as the Son of God by the gift of the Father in heaven. He realizes that Gentiles too have received the Spirit. By faith we Gentiles who have never seen Jesus may share with Peter in loving him. It is not necessary for us to have been in Galilee with Jesus. Through the witness of Peter and the other apostles we learn about what Jesus said and did. They bear witness through the Holy Spirit, and by the witness of the Spirit we are brought to know and love the living Lord' (Edmund P. Clowney).

The Christian is called upon to be self-controlled (1:13), and to rid himself of sin (2:1); in other words, holiness does not just happen, it has to be worked at. So we are urged to abstain from sinful desires (2:11) and to humble ourselves under God's mighty hand (5:6). In spite of the world's unfair attitude, we must still respect all those in authority whether they be governments or employers (2:13–20). The slave/master relationship in the first century would have been much more demanding than our twentieth-century employer/employee relationship.

Repeatedly Peter calls upon his readers to be submissive in their attitude to others (2:13, 18; 3:1; 5:5) and to be self-controlled in their personal lives (1:13; 4:7; 5:8). These are characteristics that

Peter himself was not naturally endowed with, as we see so clearly in the Gospels. But by the grace of God he learnt these things and so can we. We tend to look too much at our weaknesses and failures and conclude that we can never be holy. In the words of Dr. Lloyd-Jones:

'The main trouble with the Christian Church today is that she is too much like a clinic, too much like a hospital; that is why the great world is going to hell outside! We are all suffering – to quote Charles Lamb – "with the mumps and measles of the soul" and feeling our own pulses and talking about ourselves, and our moods and subjective states. We have lost the concept of the army of God, and the King of righteousness in this fight against the kingdom of evil . . . Holiness is a matter of service, not of feelings and subjective moods and states, not a matter of experiences. We are meant to be serving the living God with the whole of our being; and no part of us is ever meant to be used, and must not be used, in the service of sin. We must not fraternize with the enemy. That is the New Testament way of teaching holiness. What most of us need is not a clinic, but to listen to the sergeant-major drilling his troops, commanding them, warning them, threatening them, showing them what to do. The New Testament teaching is altogether different from the sentimentality and subjectivity that have controlled holiness and sanctification teaching for so long, and which tell us that it is "quite simple". But it is not easy. "Fight the good fight of faith," says the New Testament. Play the man. "Quit yourselves as men"; "Put on the whole armour of God"; "Stand in the evil day". Those are all military commands; there is nothing of the clinic about them. We must get rid of that notion of the clinic and the hospital; and we must look at these things more in terms of God and his glory, and the great campaign which he inaugurated through the Son of his love, and which he is going to bring to a triumphant conclusion.'

STUDY MATERIAL

1 Peter by Wayne Grudem (Inter-Varsity Press, 1988).
The Message of 1 Peter by Edmund Clowney (Inter-Varsity Press, 1988).

∾ 23 ∾

2 Peter

This letter was written by Peter within a year or so of the first letter and shortly before his death (1:13–14). Over the centuries, many doubts have been raised as to whether or not it was written by Peter, but the internal evidence in the epistle strongly supports Peter's authorship. Apart from 1:1, which clearly states this fact, the writer says in 1:16–18 that he was with Jesus on the mount of transfiguration.

It was probably written to the same Christians as the first letter. 'It is a letter written to people who were confronted by difficulties and by problems. The first Epistle, in the same way exactly as this Epistle, makes it quite clear that the object that the Apostle had in mind when he wrote both these letters was to comfort and to encourage and to strengthen these people. They faced difficulties, both from without and within, for their world, as one is never tired of pointing out, was a world very similar to ours' (D. M. Lloyd-Jones).

As well as persecution, the churches were now being confronted by the more serious problem of false teaching. Peter deals with this in chapter 1 by urging upon his readers a proper understanding of the preciousness of the faith which should produce in them a thoroughly Christian moral life (1:3–11). Then he reminds them of the authority of Scripture (1:12–21) on which this Christian faith rests. 'The special reason for this strong emphasis upon a sound moral life and upon the authority that buttresses it becomes clear in the last two chapters of the Epistle. Holy living had been neglected, and apostolic and scriptural authority despised, by certain false teachers. The activity of these teachers is described partly in the future tense and partly in the present. Their coming is sometimes predicted as a thing about which the readers are to be warned, and sometimes represented as already in the past. Perhaps the explanation is that the false teachers had already been active in the churches from which Peter was writing or in others with which he was acquainted, but had not yet made their way to the readers of the Epistle' (J. Gresham Machen).

CONTENTS

SUMMARY

If we are to cope with false teachers, we must be very sure about our own faith. Therefore we must make every effort to strengthen and develop our faith. Faith is something which we receive from God (1:1). Paul says that we are saved through faith, which is a gift of God (Eph. 2:8). It is the central core but not the totality of the Christian life. We must add to this God-given faith other virtues (1:5–7). 'The order in which these things are put is something which is absolutely vital. The Apostle does not ask us to do anything until he has first of all emphasised and repeated what God has done for us in Christ' (D. M. Lloyd-Jones).

What Peter is demanding from us is of the utmost importance. This is serious business, so it is not to be played at or approached casually. We are to make every effort (1:5) and this thought is repeated again in 1:10, 'Be all the more eager'. Why is this so important? Because it prevents us from being ineffective as Christians (1:8), it shows that we are not spiritually short-sighted, and it makes us spiritually strong (1:10).

Our faith is further strengthened by the reminder of the origins and foundations of Christianity. Peter therefore reminds us of the unique apostolic witness and testimony, and the authority of Scripture.

Peter then proceeds to deal with his main subject, the problem of false teachers. Chapter 2 is very similar to Jude's letter, and pulls no punches in denouncing the false teachers. These men were secretive (v.1), immoral (v.2), greedy (v.3) and arrogant (v.10). The language of 2:10–22 is devastating and Peter, like the other New Testament writers, writes with such feeling about false teachers because the truth of the gospel was at stake. This was no petty issue. These men, among other things, denied the second coming of the Lord Jesus (3:3–4). This denial was due to their deliberately ignoring certain facts (3:5); 'The ignorance was wilful, because they knew that what people of old regarded as impossible had already actually happened. Peter's argument on the facts is this. As God destroyed the old world, so God will destroy the present world. The scoffers say this is impossible. But the scoffers of old said the same thing. Nevertheless the facts of history stand out against them as a solemn warning, and for man not to believe it is just to shut his eyes to history, and to blind himself to that which has already happened' (D. M. Lloyd-Jones).

One of the unchanging marks of false teachers, whether in the first or twentieth century, is that they distort the Scriptures (3:16). They do this to their own destruction and to the destruction of all who believe them.

STUDY MATERIAL

Expository Sermons on 2 Peter by D. M. Lloyd-Jones (Banner of Truth, 1983).

ॐ 24 ॐ

John's Epistles

There is no direct reference in any of these three letters to indicate
clearly who wrote them. Tradition very strongly supports the view
that they were written by the Apostle John and there is a striking
similarity between John's Gospel and the first letter. The second
and third letters are from 'the elder'. This could refer either to the
age of the writer, or to his position in the Church. If John is the
writer, then both would be applicable. He was a very old man by
the time these letters were written (about AD 90) and he held a
leading position in the Church. It is probable that he wrote from
Ephesus to churches in the area for which he held a special love and
responsibility.

'There were many "elders" in the individual churches, but this
was "the Elder", the man who bore the title in a unique sense. It
was not unnatural that John should designate himself in the
Epistles as "Elder" rather than "Apostle". Peter also calls himself
the "fellow-elder" of the Church officers among his readers,
1 Peter 5:1. In the case of John, the title is especially suited to the
fatherly tone which is adopted in the Epistles' (J. Gresham
Machen).

1 John

Like many of the New Testament letters, 1 John has to confront
false teaching. The problem with false teaching is that it not only
denies the truth but also promotes a wrong way of living. John is
very concerned with the Christian's 'walk', that is, with his way of
living (1:5–10). Walking in the darkness is the result of loving the
world (2:15–17) and walking in the light is a consequence of

obeying the command of God (2:3–6).

John gives three reasons for writing this letter, each one promoted by a deep love and concern for his readers:

1:4	to make their joy complete
2:1	so that they will not sin
5:13	so that they may know that they have eternal life

Joy, holiness, assurance. These are the qualities John wishes to see in all Christians. Not one, but all three, and all at the same time. To lack any of these will mar fellowship, rob us of true blessing and make our Christian service ineffective. John is dealing in certainties and he continually uses the verb 'to know'.

We know God	2:3; 5:20
We know that we are in God	2:5; 4:13
We know that we are children of God	5:19
We know that we have spiritual life	3:14; 5:13

CONTENTS

1:1–10	Life and light
2:1–14	Love for fellow-Christians
15–17	Do not love the world
18–29	Warning against antichrists
3:1–24	Righteousness and love
4:1–6	Test the spirits
7–21	The love of God
5:1–21	Faith in the Lord Jesus Christ

SUMMARY

John starts with a most positive declaration that what he is about to write is not hearsay or second hand. It concerns facts about which he has direct experience (1:1–4). Here is an opening blast against the false teachers who denied the incarnation of the Lord Jesus. John says, 'We saw Him, heard Him, even touched Him (before and after His resurrection) and now we proclaim Him to you'.

It is clear that John did not believe in treading cautiously with false teachers. Their doctrine was wrong and so too was their living (1:5–10). They claimed to know God but their living denied it, and therefore their claim is a lie. Those who truly know God will keep the divine commands and walk in the light. The practical reality of this is that we are to love our fellow-believers (2:9–11) and not to love the world's standards (2:15–17).

John has a very robust concept of love. 'Christian love, according to the First Epistle of John, is not a mere sentiment; it is not the indiscriminate good-humour which is sometimes being mistaken for it today. It is compatible with the profoundest hatred of error, and the most zealous contending for the truth. There is nothing weak or sickly or effeminate about it. On the contrary, it requires an heroic mastery of selfishness and pride and passion' (J. Gresham Machen).

The greatest demonstration of love is God the Father's love for us. It is a love that is lavished upon us (3:1). 'Lavished' might seem an extravagant word, but as John goes on to describe what this love has done, it is seen to be a most appropriate word. The objective of this love is that we should be called and made children of God. In order for this to be accomplished, our sin has to be dealt with – and God's love sent Jesus to take away our sin (3:5); in other words, to destroy the devil's work (3:8). John sums it up in the great statement of 4:10, 'This is love: not that we loved God, but that he loved us and sent his Son as an atoning sacrifice for our sins'. The Authorized Version translates 'atoning sacrifice' as 'propitiation'. The word 'propitiation' means that on the cross, bearing our sin and guilt, Jesus faced the wrath of God instead of us, and paid fully on our behalf the debt that we owed to the broken law of God. On the cross, our Saviour cried, 'My God, my God, why have you forsaken me?' (Matt. 27:46). The holy God forsook His Son because He was our sin-bearer – 'God made him who had no sin to be sin for us' (2 Cor. 5:21). Jesus was 'stricken by God, smitten by him, and afflicted' (Isa. 53:4). On the cross, the Old Testament prophecy of Zechariah 13:7 was being fulfilled: 'Awake, O sword, against my shepherd,' declares the Lord Almighty. 'Strike the shepherd . . .'. The sword was the sword of judgement, and in Matthew 26:31, Jesus tells us clearly that this verse speaks of Him.

In other words, at Calvary our Lord made it possible for a holy God to be propitious – or favourably inclined – towards us, even though we were sinners and had broken His holy law. God dealt with the problem of sin in the only way that could satisfy His holy justice and enable Him to move in and break the power of Satan in sinners' lives.

John declares the greatness of God's love as an incentive to Christians to love each other (3:11; 4:7). His logic is quite simple: 'If anyone says, "I love God", yet hates his brother, he is a liar' (4:20). 'Let us not avoid the plain teaching of Scripture. If we do not love those fellow Christians whom we know well and see regularly within our fellowship circles, we cannot be loving God. We may have occasional warm feelings, but these can be merely sentimental and unrelated to other people in their real-life situations. The proof of true love is not emotion or words, but deeds, which reach out to help others in need' (David Jackman).

Many Christians have difficulty with 3:6–9 and 5:18. John is not saying that the Christian will never sin again after he is born again. That is clear from 1:8–9. We do sin and we must repent and confess that sin to God and know again the joy of forgiveness. So what do the verses in 3:6–9 mean? They 'must be read in the context of the whole letter. The present tense in the Greek verb implied habit, continuity, unbroken sequence. A Christian is quite capable of sinning. That is a sad fact of common experience, and John has named the remedy while admitting the fact. Nevertheless, opposition to sin, and hatred of it, is the ruling principle of life. A Christian may fail and fall, but the Enemy has had but brief triumph. The fallen rises again, confesses his fault, and presses on. The habitual sinner does none of these things. Just as the apostates who had left the Church proved, in John's view, that they had never belonged to it, so the one who "continues in sin", who covets no change, and seeks no victory, proves in the act that he had never known Christ. The true Christian echoes Paul: "Who shall deliver me from the body of this death? I thank God through Jesus Christ our Lord . . ."' (E. M. Blaiklock).

John defines sin as breaking the law of God (3:4) and he defines love of God as obeying His commands (5:3). To the Christian, the commands of God are not burdensome, therefore obedience is not merely a moral duty but an expression of love. Love has an emotional and moral content. 'If we judge our love purely at the emotional level, without any regard for the moral obedience which God's law demands, we may well find ourselves excusing what is in fact disobedience, because we still feel warmly towards God. Just because we do not feel self-condemned does not mean that God is smiling on us. Indeed he cannot, if we are plainly transgressing his commandments, however much we may protest that we love him or claim a special relationship with him. The God of love never indulges the sin of disobedience. All sorts of moral disasters await those who try to separate clear-cut obedience to God's law from love for him' (David Jackman).

The false teachers were playing havoc with the doctrine and therefore inevitably with the living of these Christians whom John loved so much. The result of this was a lack of confidence and certainty about their faith. John seeks to reassure them and basically gives them three tests by which they may know for themselves that they really are born of God:

The test of belief	3:23–24;	5:10, 13
The test of behaviour	1:5–7;	3:3–7
The test of fellowship	4:7–8	

2 John

John wrote this short letter to the chosen lady and her children. This could either be a Christian family or, as most modern commentators suggest, the chosen lady means a church, and her children would be the members. This figurative interpretation is encouraged by verse 13. 'The fact that it is the children who send their greetings would tend to confirm our earlier interpretation of the "lady" as a local church, and so of her sister as another local church with whom she was in fellowship' (David Jackman).

John is addressing the same problem of false teachers as in the first letter. Note again the stress on the unchanging truth (v.2), the need of love and obedience (v.6), and the warning against antichrist (v.7).

The advice given to this church is very simple. When the false teachers, who appear to be travelling preachers, visited their area, no-one was to offer them hospitality (v.10). This may appear to be a contradiction to the teaching on love in v.6, but it is not. Love means to walk in obedience to the commands of God. The false teachers were denying the deity of the Lord Jesus and it was not love to them or to those who listen to them to tolerate such heresy. In fact, it was sharing in their wicked work (v.11).

3 John

This letter is written to a Christian named Gaius, whom John obviously regards very highly (vv.2–6). The false teachers were not the only travelling preachers in the first century. Christian men who were faithful to the truth (v.8) were also moving from town to town. It is clear from the way in which John writes that these travelling evangelists had his full support and the support of their own local church. Obviously, the pagans would not help them (v.7), but Gaius had shown love and hospitality to those men (vv.5–8).

Sadly, not all in the churches were as warm and generous as Gaius. The leader of the church that Gaius belonged to, a man named Diotrephes, was vigorously opposed to the evangelists. Verses 9 and 10 are a frightening description for a man who is a leader of the church. Diotrephes's problem was not doctrinal error but personal ambition. May God deliver our churches from such men and raise up more like Gaius!

STUDY MATERIAL

The Message of John's Letters by David Jackman (Inter-Varsity Press, 1988).

✎ 25 ✎

Jude

The name 'Jude' is, in Greek, the same as 'Judas'. While there are several men with this name in the New Testament, there is little doubt that the Jude who wrote this short letter is not only the brother of James but also the brother of Jesus (see Mark 6:3). It was written about AD 65 and is a blazing condemnation of false teachers. Jude tells us in v.3 that he did not intend to write this sort of book but circumstances compelled him to defend the gospel that has been once and for all given. 'Jude brings the teaching of the entire Bible about apostasy to a tremendous climax. He takes us back to the very dawn of human history. We are reminded of apostasy at the gate of Eden and within God's ancient people Israel. Our thoughts are turned to princes and prophets, to saints and sinners, to eternal fire and everlasting darkness, to the sea and to the stars, to past judgements and future glory. We are taken into the unseen world for a strange and terrible story of fallen angels, and another story of a dispute between Michael the archangel and Satan, those antagonists who are set over against each other once more in mortal combat in Revelation 12' (S. Maxwell Coder).

In the New Testament, we have seen Jesus, Paul, Peter and John, and now Jude in their battle against false teaching. We are living in days when many believe that there is no such thing as absolute truth about God. There is only opinion, so one man's opinion is as good as the next's, therefore there can be no false teachers. But this is alien to the whole teaching of the Bible. There is such a thing as absolute truth. There is a faith which has been given once for all to the saints. False teaching is not confined to the first century. It was a problem also in the Old Testament. In Ezekiel 13, we can see the importance that God attaches to the truth, and how strongly he opposes the deniers or distorters of it. God says in v.8 of that chapter, 'I am against you'.

The mark of the false prophet is that he ignores the Bible and presents his own ideas as the Word of God. They 'prophesy out of their own imaginations' (Ezek. 13:2), and the damage that they do is horrific. According to Ezekiel 13:22, the damage is twofold: they dishearten the righteous and they encourage the wicked in their sin. False teachers, whether in Ezekiel's day or Jude's or ours, are all guilty of this and Jude, in common with all other biblical writers, denounces these men in the strongest language. This is not lack of love or bigotry but a deep concern for the glory of God and the spiritual well-being of men and women.

Jude's advice to his readers is to recognize the false teachers for what they are. They may be polite, charming and pleasant, but in reality they are godless men (v.4) and they must be opposed. The true faith is that for which Christians must contend (v.3). Contending for the faith should not make us contentious, negative or, even worse, bitter in spirit. This can easily happen, so in verses 20–23 Jude urges his readers to cultivate a spirit of love and graciousness. He reminds them that the purpose of defending the faith is not just to expose falsehood but to save men and women from the fire of God's judgement.

This letter ends with the great doxology of vv.24–25. 'As the Epistle began, so it ends, with the words of assurance for God's people living in dark days. Will they be able to keep themselves in the love of God? Can they avoid contamination in their contacts with the ungodly? Is it possible for them always to walk uprightly in the land of the living? The answer is made crystal clear. They can so live, because the One who loved them and gave Himself for them is able also to keep them from falling' (S. Maxwell Coder).

STUDY MATERIAL

Jude: The Acts of the Apostates by S. Maxwell Coder (Moody Press, 1958).

✃ 26 ✃

Revelation

'The Revelation (or the Apocalypse, as it is often called, from its opening word in the Greek) is by common consent one of the most difficult of all the books of the Bible. It is full of strange symbolism. There are curious beasts with unusual numbers of heads and horns. There are extraordinary phenomena, like the turning of one-third of the sea into blood (8:8), which are impossible to envisage. Modern readers find it strange. They are moreover not usually attracted by the fantastic schemes of prophecy which some exegetes find in it, and whose ingenuity is matched only by their improbability. The result is that for many Revelation remains a closed book' (Leon Morris).

A great many Christians would totally agree with Leon Morris in the above assessment. We feel more at home in John's Gospel, or in any other book in the New Testament, than in Revelation. The symbolism baffles us, and preachers who tell us that it is very clear, and then produce charts and amazing interpretations that cover everything from Hitler to the Common Market, frighten us away from this last book in the Bible. But it is in the Bible. It is part of inspired Scripture, so it cannot be ignored. The problem is, how do we interpret it?

There are several different approaches to interpreting Revelation. Each has its strengths and weaknesses, but basically we need to bear in mind that this book was written to Christians in particular churches at the end of the first century, and it was meant to help them face their problem. This being the case, 'We must not think of it as a kind of intellectual puzzle (spot the meaning of this symbol!) sent to a relaxed church with time on its hands and an inclination for solving mysteries. It was sent to a little, persecuted, frustrated church, one which did not know what to make of the

[126]

situation in which it found itself. John writes to meet the need of that church' (Leon Morris).

But Revelation, like all Scripture, is meant for all God's people at all times, so the lessons here are as relevant at the end of the twentieth century as they were at the end of the first century.

William Hendriksen sees the theme of the book stated completely in 17:14 – 'They will make war against the Lamb, but the Lamb will overcome them because he is the Lord of lords and King of kings – and with him will be his called, chosen and faithful followers.' This declaration of triumph is always relevant to Christians, particularly in days of weakness and little growth.

This revelation was given by Jesus Christ to John about the year AD 90, when the apostle was in exile on the island of Patmos.

CONTENTS

SUMMARY

The first three verses set the tone for everything that is to follow. This book is a revelation. The actual Greek word is 'apocalypse' and it means an unveiling of something hidden. The revelation God gave to Jesus, and Jesus gave it to John, so that John might give it to the churches. Here is a message from God for His people. 'It is a revelation or unveiling of the plan of God for the history of the world, especially of the Church. It is therefore, a direct communication from God and is not derived from any human source' (William Hendriksen).

The future of the Christian Church is inseparably linked to the person and work of the Lord Jesus Christ. The remainder of chapter 1 brings before us the glory of Christ and therefore also the glory of the Church. We are told what Christ has done for us (vv.5, 6), what he is going to do (v.7) and what he is now doing (v.8). The amazing description of Christ in 12–20 is most significant. 'The Christians were a pitiably small group, persecuted by mighty foes. To all outward appearance their situation was hopeless. But it is only as Christ is seen for what he really is that anything else can be seen for what it really is. So for these persecuted ones it was important that first of all the glory and the majesty of the risen Lord be made clear. In doing this John persistently makes use of words and concepts associated in the Old Testament with God. He does not hesitate to employ divine attributes to describe the glorious Christ' (Leon Morris).

The letters to the seven churches in chapters 2 and 3, taken as a whole, are illustrative of the Church throughout history. The lovelessness of Ephesus, the deadness of Sardis and the worldliness of Laodicea are sadly all too true of the Church at times. But thank God the faithfulness of Smyrna and the endurance of Philadelphia can also be seen from time to time. With the exception of Laodicea, Christ finds something to praise in each of the churches. But in five of the seven he also finds something to condemn. Smyrna and Philadelphia alone are unrebuked.

From the problems of the Church on earth we are taken in chapters 4 and 5 to the glories of heaven. There are many details and numbers in this vision, and clearly, as throughout Revelation, the numbers are not meant to be statistics but symbolic. 'But though the various objects which John beholds do not exist in that physical, material form, they express an important spiritual truth. They teach one main lesson. Let us not lose ourselves in our interpretation of details; let us not try to find a "deeper meaning" when there is none. We repeat: chapters 4 and 5 teach one main lesson. The picture is one; the lesson is one' (William Hendriksen). The lesson is that the Lord reigns and Christ the Lamb reigns with Him from the throne of heaven. This fact is of unspeakable comfort to Christians facing persecution and extreme difficulties. We are not in the hands of pagan powers or blind fate but of a loving Father and of the Lamb, and this secures our assurance. The scroll of chapter 5 is symbolic of the world's history in the purposes of God. The seven seals of 6:1–8:5 are symbolic of times of judgement and tribulation and the fulfilment of these purposes and plans. Sin will always reap its own consequences: war (6:2–4), famine (6:6) and death (6:8) produce their own tribulation. But notice that it is the Lamb who opens the seals, 'the suffering Lamb of God alone has the right to unleash judgements upon men: those who will not have Christ as Redeemer and Saviour must face him as Judge' (William Still). In the midst of these terrible things, God protects his Church (6:9–11).

This is brought before us more wonderfully in chapter 7. Here is 'a blessed turning to the positive and blessed side of judgement (cf. 6:9–11) for relief, to remind us that judgement serves salvation, not salvation judgement: see their proper order and priority in, e.g., Romans 9:22–23. The first verses of chapter 7 describe in graphic terms the divine restraint of natural calamities in respect of the elect, so that no satanically precipitated human disaster can interfere with their sealing unto God; see John 6:27, 2 Corinthians 1:22, Ephesians 1:13, 4:30' (William Still).

The seven trumpets (8:6–11:19) are trumpets of judgement but also trumpets of warning. This is not the final judgement of God. They indicate a 'series of happenings, that is, calamities that will occur again and again throughout this dispensation. They do not symbolize single and separate events, but they refer to woes that may be seen any day of the year in any part of the globe' (William Hendriksen). Clearly, these are judgements from God but they are also meant to warn people and call them to repentance. Sadly men prefer their sin and idolatry (9:20–21).

Men in sin are deluded and their minds blinded by Satan as part of his continuous war against God. In the next section (12:1–14:20) Satan, symbolized by the dragon together with his allies, is seen in opposition to Christ. The dragon and the beasts have great power. The first eight verses of chapter 13 are frightening. 'The chapter says little about the dragon. He remains very much in the background. He does his work not openly, but through people. John is talking about a more than human evil, but it is an evil that reveals itself in human deeds. The modern world, like the ancient, furnishes us with illustrations. Hendriksen sees the beast as signifying "world government directed against the church", and he takes the multiplicity of heads to indicate that this has various forms, as Babylon, Assyria, Rome, etc.' (Leon Morris).

Satan wars against the Church and God's people have many casualties but the emphasis of Revelation is the ultimate triumph of Christ and His Church. Final victory and judgement is in the hand of God, as we see in the rest of the book. The seven bowls of God's wrath are the final judgement that leaves no place for repentance. This final judgement of Satan and his disciples ushers in the hallelujahs of chapter 19. The vision of the rider on the white horse (19:11–16) is of Christ the warrior coming in triumph. The last battle is fought (19:19–21), Christ is victor, and the beast is destroyed. But what of Satan, the beast's master? In chapter 20 John sees Satan bound for a thousand years.

This thousand years or millennium has caused endless controversy among evangelical Christians. Basically there are three different views:

1. *Post-millennialism*. Those who hold this view teach that the second coming of Christ will follow the millennium.
2. *Pre-millennialism*. Christians who believe this teach that Christ's second coming will precede the millennium.
3. *A-millennialism or non-millennialism*. According to this view, the 'thousand years' of Revelation 20 is to be understood not literally but figuratively. The period of time which it denotes is not future but began with the finished work of Christ.

Whichever is true, ultimately we are brought to the new heaven and the new earth. 'The Apocalypse, according to any right interpretation, is a vision of final triumph. That triumph is a triumph of Christ. Behind all the lurid imagery of the book, behind the battles and the woes, and behind the glories of God's people, stands the figure of the Saviour. With him the book began, and with him, too, it ends. He is the same who lived the life of mercy and of glory on earth, the same who died for our sins on the cross. To the Lamb all power is given – all power in heaven and on earth. By him all enemies are conquered; by him the whole earth will be judged. To those who bear the mark of the beast he is an Avenger; to his Church he is an ever-living Saviour' (J. Gresham Machen).

STUDY MATERIAL

More than Conquerors by William Hendriksen (Tyndale Press, 1972).
Revelation by Leon Morris (Inter-Varsity Press, 1987).

Quotations

THE FOUR GOSPELS

William Hendriksen   *The Gospel of Matthew*, Banner of Truth, 1974, pp. 6; 46; 44

David Brown   *The Four Gospels*, Banner of Truth, 1976, p. iii

MATTHEW

D. & P. Alexander (ed.) *The Lion Handbook to the Bible*, Lion Publishing, 1973, p. 474

C. H. Spurgeon   *The Gospel of the Kingdom*, Marshall, 1893, p. 1

William Hendriksen   *The Gospel of Matthew*, Banner of Truth, 1974, p. 146

David Brown   *The Four Gospels*, Banner of Truth, 1976, pp. 15; 113.

J. Gresham Machen   *The New Testament*, Banner of Truth, 1976, p. 196

R. T. France   *The Gospel according to Matthew*, Inter-Varsity Press, 1987, pp. 291; 359

Matthew Henry   *N.T. Commentary: Matthew*, Wm Mackenzie, n.d., vol. II, p. 296

MARK

William Hendriksen   *The Gospel of Mark*, Banner of Truth, 1976, p. 13

J. Gresham Machen   *The New Testament*, Banner of Truth, 1976, p. 204

G. T. Manley (ed.)   *The New Bible Handbook*, Inter-Varsity Press, 1959, p. 331

J. C. Ryle   *Expository Thoughts on St Mark*, Clarke, 1955, p. 192

R. Alan Cole   *Mark*, Inter-Varsity Press, 1988, p. 168

LUKE

J. Gresham Machen   *The New Testament*, Banner of Truth, 1976, pp. 206; 209

Leon Morris	*Luke*, Inter-Varsity Press, 1988, p. 44
William Hendriksen	*The Gospel of Luke*, Banner of Truth, 1979, p. 250
Michael Wilcock	*The Message of Luke*, Inter-Varsity Press, 1979, p. 64
Norval Geldenhuys	*Commentary on the Gospel of Luke*, Marshall, Morgan & Scott, 1977, p. 291

JOHN

Arthur W. Pink	*Exposition of the Gospel of John*, Zondervan, 1982, p. 10
Charles Hodge	*Systematic Theology*, Nelson, 1873, vol. 1, p. 507
J. Gresham Machen	*The New Testament*, Banner of Truth, 1976, p. 222
J. C. Ryle	*Expository Thoughts on St John*, Clarke, 1976, vol. 2, p. 168
J. Douglas MacMillan	*The Lord our Shepherd*, Evangelical Press of Wales, 1986, p. 13
David Brown	*The Four Gospels*, Banner of Truth, 1976, p. 486

THE GOSPEL IN THE GOSPELS

J. Gresham Machen	*The New Testament*, Banner of Truth, 1976, p. 62
Leon Morris	*The Cross in the New Testament*, Paternoster, 1967, pp. 17; 69; 146; 150
John Brown	*Discourses and Sayings of our Lord*, Banner of Truth, 1967, vol. 1, p. 17

ACTS

J. Gresham Machen	*The New Testament*, Banner of Truth, 1976, pp. 55–6; 91; 99
J. A. Alexander	*Acts*, Banner of Truth, 1984, p. xiii
William Arnot	*Acts*, Kregel, 1978, pp. 107; 132; 460

ROMANS

J. Gresham Machen	*The New Testament*, Banner of Truth, 1976, pp. 148; 152
G. T. Manley (ed.)	*The New Bible Handbook*, Inter-Varsity Press, 1959, p. 354
Leon Morris	*Epistle to the Romans*, Inter-Varsity Press, 1988, pp. 101; 279
D. M. Lloyd-Jones	*The New Man*, Banner of Truth, 1972, p. 225

CORINTHIANS

D. & P. Alexander (ed.) *The Lion Handbook to the Bible*, Lion Publishing, 1973, pp. 587; 596

Matthew Henry — *N.T. Commentary: Corinthians*, Wm Mackenzie, n.d., vol. VI, p. 370

J. Gresham Machen — *The New Testament*, Banner of Truth, 1976, pp. 131; 140

Charles Hodge — *A Commentary on I and II Corinthians*, Banner of Truth, 1978, pp. x; 81

C. H. Spurgeon — *Morning and Evening*, Zondervan, 1965, p. 262

Donald A. Carson — *From Triumphalism to Maturity*, Inter-Varsity Press, 1986, p. 4

GALATIANS

John R. W. Stott — *The Message of Galatians*, Inter-Varsity Press, 1968, p. 185

Geoffrey B. Wilson — *Galatians*, Banner of Truth, 1979, p. 12

J. Gresham Machen — *The New Testament*, Banner of Truth, 1976, p. 129

G. T. Manley (ed.) — *The New Bible Handbook*, Inter-Varsity Press, 1959, p. 367

EPHESIANS

D. M. Lloyd-Jones — *God's Way of Reconciliation*, Evangelical Press, 1972, preface

D. M. Lloyd-Jones — *The Unsearchable Riches of Christ*, Banner of Truth, 1979, p. 13

Francis Foulkes — *Ephesians*, Inter-Varsity Press, 1983, p. 13

William Hendriksen — *New Testament Commentary: Ephesians*, Banner of Truth, 1972, pp. 72; 109

Arthur W. Pink — *Gleanings from Paul*, Moody, 1970, p. 169

PHILIPPIANS

William Hendriksen — *A Commentary on the Epistle to the Philippians*, Banner of Truth, 1963, pp. 37; 149

J. Gresham Machen — *The New Testament*, Banner of Truth, 1976, p. 175

COLOSSIANS

J. Gresham Machen — *The New Testament*, Banner of Truth, 1976, p. 164

N. T. Wright — *Colossians and Philemon*, Inter-Varsity Press, 1986, p. 103

Guy Appéré — *The Mystery of Christ*, Evangelical Press, 1984, p. 86

D. M. Lloyd-Jones — *Studies in the Sermon on the Mount*, Inter-Varsity Press, 1959, vol. 1, p. 16

THESSALONIANS
F. F. Bruce   *Paul and His Converts*, Lutterworth, 1965, p. 25
J. Gresham Machen   *The New Testament*, Banner of Truth, 1976, p. 118
Leon Morris   *First and Second Thessalonians*, Inter-Varsity Press, 1984, pp. 50; 123

TIMOTHY
John R. W. Stott   *The Message of 2 Timothy*, Inter-Varsity Press, 1973, pp. 13; 115
William Hendriksen   *First and Second Timothy*, Banner of Truth, 1957, pp. 199; 263

PHILEMON
William Hendriksen   *A Commentary on the Epistle to Philemon*, Banner of Truth, 1974, p. 209

HEBREWS
D. & P. Alexander (ed.) *The Lion Handbook to the Bible*, Lion Publications, 1973, p. 626
Raymond Brown   *The Message of Hebrews*, Inter-Varsity Press, 1982, pp. 14; 91
Arthur W. Pink   *Hebrews*, Baker, 1975, p. 27
D. M. Lloyd-Jones   *The Final Perseverance of the Saints*, Banner of Truth, 1975, p. 326
P. E. Hughes   *Hebrews*, Eerdman, 1977
Geoffrey B. Wilson   *Hebrews*, Banner of Truth, 1970, p. 81
Leon Morris   *The Cross in the New Testament*, Paternoster, 1967, p. 296

JAMES
J. Gresham Machen   *The New Testament*, Banner of Truth, 1976, pp. 234; 238
Douglas J. Moo   *James*, Inter-Varsity Press, 1986, p. 36
Alec Motyer   *The Message of James*, Inter-Varsity Press, 1985, p. 82

PETER
Edmund P. Clowney   *The Message of 1 Peter*, Inter-Varsity Press, 1988, pp. 22; 54
Wayne Grudem   *1 Peter*, Inter-Varsity Press, 1988, p. 9
J. Gresham Machen   *The New Testament*, Banner of Truth, 1976, p. 253
D. M. Lloyd-Jones   *The New Man*, Banner of Truth, 1972, p. 174
D. M. Lloyd-Jones   *Expository Sermons on 2 Peter*, Banner of Truth, 1983, p. 1

JOHN'S EPISTLES

J. Gresham Machen   *The New Testament*, Banner of Truth, 1976, p. 265

David Jackman   *The Message of John's Letters*, Inter-Varsity Press, 1988, pp. 132; 140; 187

E. M. Blaiklock   *Faith is the Victory*, Paternoster, 1957, p. 41

JUDE

S. Maxwell Coder   *Jude, The Acts of the Apostates*, Moody, 1958, p. 121

REVELATION

Leon Morris   *The Book of Revelation*, Inter-Varsity Press, 1987, pp. 22; 53; 161

William Hendriksen   *More than Conquerors*, Tyndale Press, 1972, pp. 82; 116; 182

William Still   *And I Saw*, Didasko Press, 1988, pp. 41; 45

J. Gresham Machen   *The New Testament*, Banner of Truth, 1976, p. 283

General Index

A number of authors and their works are listed in this index. In most cases the works are sets of commentaries or sermons; wherever this is so, the works are listed in the order in which their subjects appear in the New Testament, i.e. Matthew before Mark, Timothy before Titus, and so on; all other items are in alphabetical order.

Scripture Index

In the interest of brevity, this index lists only those verses which are cited out of their immediate contexts. Within the 'summaries' to the New Testament books, the practice has been to index chapters, or groups of chapters rather than verses. Verses from the various lists and tables are not included, since the subject matter of the lists can be approached through the General Index.

16.17	9	12.16–21	26
22.28	63	13.1–5	26
25.41	26	15.11–32	28–9
25.44	26	15.11–20	15
26–8	8	16.19–31	26
26.28	29	18.13	15
26.31	120	19.2	15
27.46	120	19.41	15
		20–24	17
Mark		20.9–18	26
1	10–11	20.35,37	30
1.1	1	22.42	15
1.15	28	23.34	29
2–3	11	23.43	15
2.14	4	24.13	15
3.17	9–10	24.47	29
5.37	9		
5.41	10		
5.42	9	**John**	
6–8	11	1–2	20
6.3	124	1.14	18
7.2–4	9	1.29	27
9	12	3–5	20
9.29	11	3.8	30
10	12	3.16	26, 30–1
10.45	27		
11.21	9	5.24	30
13.33	11	5.28–9	30
14.37	12	6–7	20–1
14.38	11	6.27	129
16.7	9	6.37–44	30
		6.44	30
Luke		7.5	107
1–3	14–15	8–9	21
1.3	15	8.58	19
1.3–4	13	10	21
2.11	25	10.11	28
3.1–2	13	10.18	28
4–7	15–16	10.28–9	30
5.20,24	29	11–12	21–2
5.27–8	4	11.50	28
6.23	30	13–17	19,22
7.47	29	14.8	28
9–19	16	15.13	27,28
9.25	30	15.15	85
10.31	15	18.14	28
11.4	29	20.30	18
12.10	29	20.31	18

[145]